THE VANISHING WETLANDS

THE VANISHING

WETLANDS

**TRENT
DUFFY**

AN IMPACT BOOK
FRANKLIN WATTS

New York ■ Chicago ■ London ■ Toronto ■ Sydney

Frontis: The Everglades

Photographs copyright ©: Animals Animals/Earth Scenes: pp. 2 (Esther Kiviat), 20 (Bates Littlehales), 105 (Esther Kiviat); Dean Spaulding: pp. 15, 17, 25, 28, 55, 60, 64, 69, 74; Photo Researchers, Inc.: pp. 36 (F. Gohier), 137 (Jeff Lepore); Hamblin/Powell: pp. 42, 48, 52, 58, 78, 82; Comstock/Georg Gerster: p. 108; Visuals Unlimited: pp. 113 (Martin G. Miller), 124 (D. Newman); Arcata National Wildlife Sanctuary: p. 117.

Library of Congress Cataloging-in-Publication Data

Duffy, Trent.
   The vanishing wetlands / Trent Duffy.
      p.   cm.—(An Impact book)
   Includes bibliographical references (p.   ) and index.
   ISBN 0-531-13034-7
   1. Wetlands—Juvenile literature.   2. Wetland ecology—United States—Juvenile literature.   3. Wetland conservation—United States—Juvenile literature.   4. Wetland fauna—United States—Juvenile literature.   5. Wetland plants—United States—Juvenile literature.   6. Man—Influence on nature—United States—Juvenile literature. [1. Wetlands. 2. Wetland ecology. 3. Ecology. 4. Conservation of natural resources.] I. Title.
QH87.3.D54   1994
574.5'26325—dc20   93-26332   CIP   AC

ACKNOWLEDGMENTS

Among the many people who provided assistance and support during the writing of this book, I'd especially like to thank my editor, Victoria Mathews; Dean T. Spaulding; Anne Cherry; and Frances and Howard Kiernan.

CONTENTS

INTRODUCTION

Little more than a generation ago, swamps and other wetlands were generally considered dank, useless places that served as breeding grounds for mosquitoes and even disease. If these areas weren't drained for agricultural, residential, or commercial development, Americans saw no purpose for them—except as dumping grounds for old refrigerators, tires, and cars.

All that has begun to change. Today many people, including scientists, environmentalists, bird watchers, hunters, and others, recognize the value of the nation's wetlands and the importance of saving them. However, it has been difficult to persuade everyone of the need to save natural areas that were once ignored, if not scorned. In fact, there are those who believe that wetlands regulations have been applied too zealously, and that the rights of property owners and others have been overlooked.

Quite a few people still do not really understand what wetlands are. This book will explain the various types of wetlands, why they're important, and the kinds of plants and animals that live in them. It will also look at the volatile issue of wetlands preservation, showing how shifting government policies and priorities have left some landowners confused and angry.

WHAT ARE WETLANDS?

As the name would lead you to expect, wetlands are natural habitats where "water is the primary factor controlling the environment and the associated plant and animal life."[1] They range in size from less than an acre to thousands of square miles. Wetlands occur at or near the edges of rivers, lakes, bays, and other bodies of water. Under natural conditions, most bodies of water don't have precisely defined edges, since water levels fluctuate with levels of precipitation, the time of the year, and, on the coasts, with tides. Any area that is sometimes covered with water and other times is not is generally considered a wetland. These wetlands are transitional environments that are found between bodies of water on one side and uplands (the term used for land that isn't wetland) on the other.

Wetlands also occur where the water table is close to ground level. While the most recognizable wetlands are swamps and marshes that may include areas of brackish water fringed by cattails and other reeds, a wetland may also be an open meadow, a forest, or a brush-filled field—in these cases, it's the fact that the water table is at or near the surface that determines wetland status.

The plant life of wetlands differs from that of upland environments. Wetlands are dominated by hydrophytes, plants that can tolerate the presence of water at their roots for a significant period of time. These ecosystems are also characterized by soil types that differ from those found in uplands.

The three main types of wetlands are marshes, swamps, and bogs. Wetlands are dynamic ecosystems teeming with plant and animal life. Flood control is but one of their benefits to us. (We'll examine the kinds of wetlands and their importance in chapters 1 and 2.)

SOME HISTORY

People have viewed wetlands with disdain for thousands of years. From Roman times, humans have been draining swamps to control mosquitoes and malaria. Wetlands were considered wastelands when European settlers arrived in the United States. George Washington himself was involved in an effort to drain the Great Dismal Swamp on the Virginia–North Carolina border in the early 1760s. And as one writer observed recently, a century later, wetlands remained a threatening presence:

> *In 1876 the president of the American Public Health Association declared, "The state cannot afford to be indifferent to" the presence of swamps "because they check production, limit population, and reduce the standard of health and vigor."*[2]

Such attitudes have persisted through much of this century. The federal government continued to subsidize the conversion of many wetlands to farmland until very recently. An estimated 60 million acres (24.3 million hectares) of wetlands were modified for agricultural use between 1940 and 1960 alone. All too often, wetlands have been drained of water and filled in to provide sites for homes, industrial parks, condominium complexes, or even airports or football stadiums. Conversely, they've been dredged (had soil removed, so the water reached a greater depth) to improve navigation or to build marinas. Wetlands that haven't been so altered have frequently become dumping places for garbage.

The United States Fish and Wildlife Service estimates that there were 221 million acres (89.4 million hectares) of wetlands in the lower forty-eight states at the time of the Revolutionary War; of those, 105 million acres (42.5 million hectares), or less than half, survive today.[3] During the past two centuries, the state of New Hampshire has lost only 9 percent of its wetlands. However, in the rest of the continental United States, wetland loss has ranged from 20 to 91 percent.

Seven midwestern states—Illinois, Indiana, Iowa, Michigan, Minnesota, Ohio, and Wisconsin—account for more than 35 million acres (14.2 million hectares) of lost wetlands. It should be kept in mind that the loss of the majority of midwestern wetlands has had a positive effect: draining these acres exposed some of the richest soils in the world, which were then put to good use in this fertile agricultural region.

Now that public perception about the value of wetlands is changing, the United States is scrambling to preserve many of its remaining wetlands. But, while estimates vary, as many as 1,000 acres (400 hectares) of wetlands are still lost every day.

Wetlands can be found in every state, including Hawaii and the desert states of the West. Alaska has more wetlands than the lower forty-eight states combined: 170 million acres (68.8 million hectares)—most of it frozen tundra—as compared with 105 million (42.5 million hectares). It also leads the union in the *percentage* of territory that is still wetland. Other states with a high percentage of wetland territory are Florida, Louisiana, Maine, New Jersey, and North Carolina; in terms of *actual acreage*, Florida, Louisiana, Minnesota, and Texas follow Alaska.

These habitats are also widely distributed throughout Canada, which contains nearly 25 percent of the world's wetlands, including most of its peat bogs.

1

THE TYPES OF WETLANDS

Technically, a wetland is an area that is "inundated or saturated by surface or groundwater at a frequency and duration sufficient to support . . . a prevalence of vegetation typically adapted for life in saturated soil conditions."[1] Because the soil is flooded or saturated for long periods during the growing season, it is called hydric soil. The hydrophytes that constitute the major portion of plants growing in wetlands have adapted well to hydric soil, which is a soil deficient in oxygen. Other plants are dependent on absorbing larger quantities of oxygen through their root systems.

Wetlands are generally categorized as swamps, marshes, or bogs, but for several reasons precise categorization can be difficult. Each type of wetland shares some characteristics with other types. One type can abut or be surrounded by another—for instance, a small bog can lie within the borders of a larger swamp. Or, to cite a very prominent example, the Florida Everglades, the largest wetland in the continental United States, contains marsh and swamp areas (this unique ecosystem is described in chapter 5).

In addition, some experts use other broad categories to classify wetlands. For example, wetlands can be

13

classified first as coastal (tidal) or inland (nontidal), and then assigned to various subsidiary categories. Coastal wetlands themselves can be saltwater *or* freshwater, but inland wetlands are always freshwater.

MARSHES

Marshes are dominated by grasses and other soft-stemmed plants that don't grow much higher than an adult male. If you can get close to a typical marsh plant, such as a cattail, sedge, or reed, and press the stem, there will be a little give. There are more likely to be areas of open water in a marsh than in other wetlands. Marshes are commonly found near the mouths of rivers (especially those with deltas) and alongside rivers, lakes, and oceans. However, they can also be found in isolated basins far from the nearest pond or stream. Like swamps (which are dominated by trees), marshes are complex ecosystems full of plants and animals that have adapted to living in an environment that has features of both land and water.

The water level in marshes may fluctuate widely: some marshes are always saturated, with water that may be as deep as 3 feet (1 m). (Most plants that are adapted to wetland conditions cannot grow when the water level exceeds 3 feet—these areas usually turn into open water.) Other marshes may have standing water only during the rainier parts of the year or while snows melt and run off into their shallow basins.

COASTAL MARSHES
Saltwater Marshes ▪ Most common on the East Coast, saltwater marshes develop at river mouths, behind dunes, and in shallow areas close to the sea, especially on the edges of estuaries and intertidal flats.

Estuaries are areas where salt and fresh water mix. Ocean tides bring salt water with them, but estuaries

14

A freshwater marsh in New Hampshire sits alongside wooded uplands.

also get a continual infusion of fresh water at their inland end. This results in a complex and diverse ecosystem, one that frequently includes a mixture of salt- and freshwater marshes. The largest estuary in the United States is the Chesapeake Bay, and San Francisco Bay is the biggest estuary on the West Coast; wetlands in both areas are among those most threatened by pollution and development.

Intertidal flats, which are sometimes called mud flats, are the areas where tides rise too high to allow saltwater marsh vegetation to grow.[2] They're home to a multitude of small invertebrates like ghost shrimp and gaper clams, as anyone who has explored the coastline at low tide can attest. (If you've ever done this, you will also remember the distinctive odor of intertidal flats.) Some ecologists classify these areas as nonvegetated wetlands.

In all coastal saltwater marshes, the grasses and reeds that flourish have adapted to salt water. Where the land is flat, saltwater marshes can stretch some distance in from shore, carrying with them the distinctive smells of the sea. Such vegetation cannot grow, however, where the land is subject to strong currents or the full force of the surf.

Coastal saltwater marshes account for less than 5 percent of the wetlands in the United States today. (In subtropical and tropical areas, tidal saltwater marshes are replaced by mangrove swamps; see page 23.)

Freshwater Coastal Marshes ▪ Only about 1 percent of the wetlands in America are freshwater coastal marshes. Although these form inland from salt marshes and mangrove swamps, they are still affected by ocean tides. Dominated by shrubs, grasses, and floating-leaved aquatic plants such as water lilies, these wetlands are found in bays and inlets, as well as in the inland portion of estuaries.

INLAND FRESHWATER MARSHES
Freshwater marshes, which make up about 25 percent of America's wetlands, form alongside rivers (especially in their floodplains, the nearby low-lying areas that are flooded when the river overflows its banks) or at the edges of lakes and ponds. They also form on their own, whenever basins receive enough runoff from surrounding uplands or sit above a high water table. These marshes may be classified as shallow or deep, depending on an average water level, while allowing for the fact that water levels in most wetlands

The skyline of Atlantic City hovers over the Edwin B. Forsythe National Wildlife Refuge, a coastal marsh.

fluctuate seasonally or annually. The soil of some marshes is always waterlogged; others are dry for months.

Grasses, sedges, and rushes are all typical marsh plants. While much of this soft-stemmed vegetation looks alike, the species are in fact highly varied. Botanists divide them into three categories, based on the plant's relation to the water.

1) Emergents are plants that grow partly in and partly out of the water; they exist in both shallow and deep marshes. Most sedges, such as cattails and bulrushes, are emergents.

17

2) Floating aquatics are deep-marsh plants. Some float freely on the surface, with no roots at all, such as water hyacinth. Others, such as water lilies, are rooted in mucky soil; a long leaf stalk called a petiole extends to the surface where leaves and flowers sit. This petiole can be 5 or 6 feet long (1.5 or 1.8 m), so these floating aquatics are found in much deeper water than emergents; they can even dot ponds and other areas of open water.

3) Submergents are also rooted in the marsh or pond bottom, but their leaves may be underwater as well; the carnivorous bladderwort is one example.[3]

Deep marshes tend to be permanently covered with 2 to 4 feet of water, while shallow marshes are not as flooded, with less than 1 foot of water during the growing season. (Again, these averages are subject to variation.) Shallow marshes often appear right alongside deep ones, on the landward (upland) side. In these situations, the types of plants provide a visual cue that distinguishes between the two. The shallow marsh may feature a ribbon of emergents mixed in with plants that are more typical of uplands, while as the water gets deeper, the emergents predominate and eventually start sharing the space with aquatics and submergents.

Wet Meadows ▪ Another type of freshwater marsh is the wet meadow. Most of the year, wet meadows, which to the untrained eye look virtually identical to grasslands, have saturated soil. They're flooded seasonally, if at all. Wet meadows are common in the Southeast and in both forested and nonforested mountain regions.

Riparian Wetlands ▪ If you live in an urban or suburban area where homes and businesses close to a river are periodically flooded, chances are they are built on what was a riparian wetland. Left in their natural state, these marshes alongside rivers serve as floodplains to absorb temporarily high waters. Riparian wetlands exist even in arid sections of western North America. While the marshes alongside western rivers may have very dry soil for most of the year, their greenery is in decided contrast to the upland vegetation. (Riparian wetlands that are forested are classified as swamps.)

Prairie Potholes ▪ Prairie potholes are a special kind of marsh that developed after the end of the last Ice Age. As the glaciers retreated, they left behind irregular terrain with soil that drained poorly. Each spring, as snow melted, water collected in the depressions, promoting the growth of temporary, seasonal marshes. Nowadays these depressions are found in four states in the upper Midwest (North Dakota, which has the most prairie potholes; Iowa; Minnesota; and South Dakota) and the Canadian provinces of Manitoba, Ontario, and Saskatchewan.

Prairie potholes receive almost all their water from rain or thawing snow. While some have surface water year-round, the majority run dry at some point in the year. The water level also dips in years of drought. In fact, in dry years these areas can rapidly become dominated by upland plants, and some are even farmed without any extensive preparatory work such as draining.

Over the last century, half of the prairie potholes in North Dakota have been lost, as well as a higher proportion in surrounding areas; this has been due mostly to agricultural drainage. This loss has had an enor-

As each winter's snows melt, water collects in thousands of prairie potholes dotting the upper Midwest and the Prairie Provinces.

mous impact on waterfowl populations because, depending on the year, 50 to 80 percent of all the ducks in North America breed there.[4]

Ducks need ample food and an environment that is relatively safe from predators in order to breed successfully. Now that there are fewer potholes, there is more competition for food, and individual wetlands may be host to more species, including animals that prey on ducklings. Studies have also shown that ducks may stop at several different potholes in the upper Midwest or Canada during the breeding season. The snow in a tiny temporary pothole will begin to thaw in late winter, for example, providing the first feeding site for the birds. Later, in the spring, they will move on to the wetland vegetation at the edge of a nearby permanent or semipermanent pothole to nest and lay eggs.

HOW MARSHES DEVELOP

Many marshes form over the course of hundreds of years as fallen leaves and other decomposing vegetation fill in ponds or small lakes. Once the dead leaves and other organic matter settle on the bottom of a pond, submergents can root. As the level of sediment gradually increases, emergent plants are the next to root. While this mixture of hydrophytes grows, the area eventually becomes a bona fide marsh. This process involves temporary setbacks—for instance, a few wet years in succession could cause water levels to rise and kill off the emergents.

Poorly drained shallow depressions alongside rivers or streams are another place where marshes occur. These areas absorb much of the excess water when the river overflows its banks during the late-winter thaw or after heavy rains.

Marshes are also typically found at deltas at river mouths; most of the largest rivers in the world, including the Mississippi, the Nile, and the Danube, have marshes in their deltas. Upstream, erosion from surface soils of the river's basin is carried along as sediment by the swift-flowing water. However, as the river approaches sea level, the ground becomes flatter, so the gradient and the water speed decrease. The sediment is deposited, and, over the course of tens of thousands of years, the sediment accumulates until land is built up into a delta. As the process continues, the new marshes are a step toward the creation of more delta land.

SWAMPS

Swamps are the dominant wetland type in the United States, accounting for about two-thirds of the nation's wetland acreage. Shrubs and trees are the plant species that dominate a swamp, in contrast to the soft-stemmed grasses and reeds that proliferate in marshes. The trees that tend to flourish in swamps can tolerate wet soils that upland forest species cannot. Beneath them, at ground level, shrubs such as spicebush and sweet pepperbush grow alongside the skunk cabbage, which is usually the first plant to appear each spring.

Water levels that fluctuate greatly and mineral soils that drain poorly characterize swamp sites, as they do most wetlands. Swamps sometimes act as transitional zones between marshes and upland forests, and to an untrained eye they often resemble the forests of the surrounding uplands.

Let's look at the various types of swamps in Canada and the United States.

NORTHERN SWAMPS

Swamps in the northern half of the continent are often classified by the dominant type of tree. Red maple swamps are perhaps the most common, although deciduous conifers such as northern white cedar and tamarack can also prevail. (It should be noted that red maple trees, which of all the tree species found in the eastern half of the United States have the farthest reach from north to south, are very common in mixed hardwood forests throughout uplands also.) Black spruce, white spruce, or balsam fir dominate in coniferous northern swamps. Floodplain forests, which occur in poorly drained lowland sites along such rivers as the Connecticut and the upper Mississippi, are characterized by black willows, cottonwoods, and silver maples.

SOUTHERN SWAMPS

In the warmer, southern sections of the United States, different species of trees dominate swamps. Foremost among them are the bald cypress and the pond cypress, both of which are actually in the redwood family. These trees lend their name to the cypress swamps occurring in the Southeast. Two of the most prominent cypress swamps are the Okefenokee Swamp in Georgia and the Big Cypress Swamp, just to the west of the Everglades. In the Great Dismal Swamp, the bald cypress mingles with typical hardwoods, like the red maple, characteristic of northern swamps.

Southern bottomland hardwood swamps originally covered much of the coastal plain of the Southeast and fringed major rivers, including the Mississippi. A major part of these bottomlands has been converted to farmland over the past two centuries. The bald cypress is often found in those wetlands that remain, along with the tupelo, overcup oak, sweetgum, and red maple.

Mangrove Swamps ▪ In subtropical and tropical parts of the world, mangrove swamps replace coastal salt marshes. They are named after their most conspicuous plant, the mangrove, one of the rare trees that can tolerate salt water at its roots. These wetlands fringe most of the coastal areas of the Everglades and can also be found in Hawaii, Louisiana, and Texas.

SHRUB SWAMPS

Shrub swamps are often transitional in nature. Over the course of hundreds of years, a marsh or a sedgy meadow may fill in and become a shrub swamp; gradually, trees begin to grow and can eventually replace shrubs as the dominant vegetation. Where shrub wetlands are long-lived, however, the nature of the soil or weather conditions often discourage tree growth.

While small shrub swamps are found throughout North America, they are most common and larger in the upper Midwest and the Southeast. Thickets of alder and pussy willows prevail, providing a dense cover for a variety of wildlife.

A pocosin is a more permanent shrub swamp, found only in Virginia and the Carolinas. Its name comes from the Algonquin word for "swamp on a hill" and, indeed, pocosins tend to form in elevated spots between streams. Pond pine and hollies are typical dominant species.[5]

WESTERN SWAMPS
Many wetlands scientists consider the cottonwood-willow forests that form in the river valleys of the arid Southwest to be swamps. (The Verde River in central Arizona is flanked by such areas.) These wetlands differ from those in other parts of the country in two vital ways. First, most of their water supply comes from short, intense floods that occur only intermittently; thus, these forests are adapted to periods of both intense wetness and dryness. Second, the soils do not match the typical wetlands soils (based on eastern prototypes), partly because much more fresh sediment is dumped during floods, and it then covers the underlying wetland soil.[6] One other type of wetland found in the West that should be mentioned is the bosque, or mesquite forest.

BOGS

Bogs are very unusual ecosystems characterized by wet, spongy, very poorly drained soil. The soil itself is often peaty. Like other wetlands, bogs are rich in unusual plants, most of which have made unique adaptations to survive in a wetland environment. Unlike swamps and marshes, however, bogs do not serve as

Plants in bogs make adaptations in order to live on a quaking mat of Sphagnum moss. A small pond sits in the center of this 15-acre mat.

habitat for any significant amount of wildlife. While bogs and associated peatlands cover large areas of northern Minnesota, they still account for less than 5 percent of the wetlands in the United States.

To understand bogs, we must look at how they were formed. In North America, bogs occur mostly in areas of the Northeast, Midwest, and Canada that were covered by glaciers during the last Ice Age. As the ice cover retreated at the end of that era, it dragged stones with it, some of which were big enough to gouge out depressions. Bergs of ice also broke off from the main body of the glacier, settling in other depressions. Either from ice melting or from rainwater, these depressions then filled in with water; geologists call them glacial ponds or lakes, and many of them survive today.

If the water in these ponds had a low mineral content, they were colonized by Sphagnum mosses, a genus containing more than 300 species of gray-green moss. As these and other plants (notably heaths such as leatherleaf) decayed, a layer of peat formed, building up very slowly over time. Meanwhile, Sphagnum moss continued to grow on top of the water. It absorbed what minerals there were in the already mineral-poor water, replacing them with acids; the result was very acidic water.

In order for glacial ponds or lakes to change slowly into bogs, one more condition was necessary—there had to be no way for water to drain out of them. In addition to lacking outlets, most of these depressions also had no inlets supplying fresh water. The only infusion of water came from rainwater, which has no dissolved air. Because there is no dissolved oxygen in the water of the bog, carbon dioxide accumulates in it; this in turn tends to prevent the growth of microscopic flora.[7]

The unique water chemistry of bogs—this combination of mineral-poor, oxygen-deprived, and acidic water—means that these microscopic flora, such as bacteria and fungi, are almost totally absent. Since they are essential to the decomposition of organic matter, dead Sphagnum moss and other plants decay at a much slower rate than normal, and beds of peat gradually accumulate beneath the surface. As the layers of peat thicken and the new Sphagnum mosses grow on the surface, a quaking mat forms.

If all open water has been covered, the bog may look from a distance like a very flat meadow. Nonetheless, it's still a quaking mat under which clear water remains. While a mature floating bog may be thick enough to support a person's weight, walking on one is like walking on a wet sponge: the pressure of your feet causes you to sink into the mat a bit, and water begins to accumulate in your footprints. (*Caution:* Do not try to walk on a bog unless a sign or a park ranger says it's all right. Not all bogs will support a person's weight, and appearances can be deceiving. Also, a bog is a very fragile ecosystem—it can take many years for the depressions that footprints make to fill in enough to disappear.)

The peat that accumulates in a bog can be harvested, dried, and then burned as fuel, as is still common in some rural parts of Ireland.

These same unique factors also account for the limited kinds of plants that thrive in bogs. Leatherleaf (an evergreen in the heath family), various flowering orchids, and the water willow (actually a loosestrife) are among the plants most commonly found interspersed with the Sphagnum mosses on a bog's quaking mat. Compared to their counterparts upland in the deciduous forest, those shrubs found in bogs have undergone modifications. For instance, because the water at root level is so highly acidic that it can't readily be absorbed, these plants often have a different leaf shape

Organic matter decomposes very slowly in a bog.
At Chickering Bog in Vermont, a Nature Conservancy
volunteer pulls up a 100-year-old fence post to show
how little the buried portion has decayed compared to
the area exposed to the air.

to prevent water loss via evaporation or to capture rainwater. Also of note are carnivorous plants, such as the pitcher plant, the sundew, and the butterwort.

Cranberry, the only bog species to have been domesticated, is indigenous to the United States. Bogs are so well suited to its growth that they are still used extensively for commercial cultivation of the tasty berry.

In rare instances, where there is very little standing water under the mat, small trees can grow in the middle of a bog. But for the most part, the trees that grow there are generally found on the outer fringes of the bog; they first decrease in height and then disappear altogether toward the center. Where there are trees, they're generally evergreens—most notable the black, or bog, spruce (a source of both chewing gum and spruce beer in the nineteenth century). Since coniferous trees do not drop all their leaves annually—or expend energy to make new ones—they are better adapted for any habitat, such as a bog, where nutrients are in short supply. Another tree that, while abundant in northern upland forests, prefers bogs is the tamarack, or larch. This deciduous conifer sheds its needles every year. Its wood has been used in making small craft from pre-Columbian times up to the present day.

While most of the wildlife found in bogs visits from surrounding uplands, there are a few characteristic species of bog animals. Among them are amphibians, especially the rare Pine Barrens treefrog and the bog, or Muhlenberg's, turtle, and butterflies.

Bogs have proved to be valuable laboratories for ecologists, geologists, and archaeologists. Not only does the absence of bacteria slow down decomposition but the acidic water that permeates the peat is also a natural embalming fluid. Fossil pollens preserved in the peat provide a record of plant growth in the surrounding area from 10,000 to 15,000 years ago. Human bodies found in bogs are usually very well preserved and thus of major importance to scientists. When the so-called Lindow Man was discovered in a bog near Manchester, England, in 1964, his body was so well preserved, even after some 2,000 years, that scientists were able to determine not only his age and the cause of death but also what he had eaten for his last meal!

Fens are the other major type of peatland. They differ from bogs in that they receive some amount of both surface water and groundwater. Because they receive some nutrient-rich water, they can be slightly more fertile than bogs, and grasses and sedges often replace Sphagnum moss as the dominant species.

There are also bogs in poorly drained depressions in the tropics, where peat is formed almost entirely from tree remains. (Glacial activity is obviously not a factor in the ecological development of these areas.)

HABITAT DYNAMICS

Perhaps the most important thing to keep in mind when visiting or even reading about wetlands is that they are remarkably unstable environments. As part of the natural cycle, wetlands can change form over the years: what was a marsh can become a wet prairie; what was a bog can become a wet forest; what was a shallow pond can become a marsh. As mentioned earlier, the classification of one wetland as a swamp rather than a marsh, or as a bog rather than a fen, can be based on minute differences. Changes in water depth, herbivore activity, topography, or other factors from one year to the next can alter the look—and even the classification—of a wetland.

While a wetland evolves, the plants and wildlife in the ecosystem will change as well. For instance, a slightly lower water level in a marsh might encourage the growth of red maple and other swamp-tolerant trees. When the trees increase and mature, they shade out marsh plants that need a lot of light to survive. Eventually, as this long process of marsh-transforming-into-swamp continues, marsh-loving animals such as the muskrat will leave for a more hospitable environment.

THE LAKE THAT FINALLY LIVED UP TO ITS NAME

We are used to the landscape around us being altered by devastating natural events such as hurricanes or by human activity such as development, but the instability of wetlands takes some getting used to. We have not been trained to appreciate the naturally slow evolution of some habitats—after all, a lake or an upland forest looks basically the same from year to year. In fact, however, one scientist who studies marshes has observed that their instability—whether the result of fire, drought, or flooding—is generally beneficial.[8]

An Iowa marsh provides a good example of the fluid nature of wetland conditions. Little Wall Lake in central Iowa was a shallow freshwater marsh of about 250 acres (101 hectares). (In the prairie pothole region some marshes are locally called lakes, a result, perhaps, of their water levels' being abnormally high when they were first discovered.) It had been dry at least four times between the end of the nineteenth century and the 1950s; during these natural droughts, the plants and wildlife in the marsh changed somewhat, as those species unable to adapt to the arid conditions died out.

In wetter years, sedges, cattails, and other aquatic plants dominated a shallow marsh with some patches of open water. This wetland was visited by innumerable birds, muskrat, mink, and midges. In 1953, part of the marsh was dredged to provide a larger area of open water, which was then used by boaters. By the mid-1960s, authorities had raised the lake level farther and inundated all vegetation. Little Wall Lake became a true lake at last, and recreational activity flourished. However, now only a few birds stop there in migration, and waterfowl no longer breed there.[9]

ENERGY FLOW

A basic pattern common to all natural ecosystems is energy flow, the movement of chemical energy up a food chain, from plants to herbivores to carnivores. In wetlands, there are two major energy-flow patterns. The grazing food chain involves the consumption of green plants directly by plant eaters; plant eaters are then the food source for larger animals higher up the chain. The detrital food chain involves those organisms that depend primarily on detritus, or organic debris, as their food source. In the detrital food chain, dead organic matter from plants, broken down by bacteria and fungi, is the major food source for worms and aquatic insects. Those small animals are then eaten in turn by larger insects, birds, and mammals.

In wetlands, the two energy-flow patterns often overlap. For instance, the muskrat is a rodent relatively high up on the food chain, eating both plants and small freshwater animals, such as mussels, crayfish, and salamanders. But muskrats also shred vegetation as they build their lodges, in the process exposing more surface area of dead vegetation. The greater surface area increases the amount of organic matter on which bacteria and other decomposers in the detrital food chain can work.

In breaking down detritus, decomposers release mineral nutrients and soluble organic compounds back into the wetland. As a result, these ecosystems don't need fertilizers, the way farmlands do, to be productive. And in scientific terms, wetlands are extremely productive places. When biologists measure productivity—the total living output of plants and animals in an ecosystem—wetlands are near the top of the list. The principal reasons for the high productivity of wetlands are:

1) The way the grazing and detrital food chains work to complement each other;

2) The high level of photosynthesis occurring as plants take in and store the sun's energy, thus beginning the food chain;

3) The efficient recycling of nutrients; and

4) The periodic rise and fall of the water level, which allows nutrients to be brought in from other ecosystems by flooding or to be made more accessible to other organisms when the water level recedes.

While wetlands left in their natural state don't have the same immediate impact on human life as do the rich agricultural lands that supply us with most of the food we eat, their high productivity is still vitally important, as we'll discover in the next chapter.

2

THE IMPORTANCE OF WETLANDS

Today Americans and Canadians appreciate and value their wetlands far more than they did a generation ago. Yet the need to overcome old stereotypes about wastelands and dumping grounds persists. Let's look at the different functions wetlands provide for humans.

BIODIVERSITY

American wetlands are home to a vast array of species, many of them rare, threatened, or endangered. It is estimated that 75 percent of North American bird species use wetlands for resting, feeding, and/or nesting; among ducks and other waterfowl the percentage is perhaps higher. Two-thirds of the fish and shellfish harvested commercially in the United States come from species that depend on wetlands for all or part of their life cycles.[1] These biologically diverse environments are also home to a wide variety of amphibians, insects, and plants.

Some people question the wisdom of maintaining this biodiversity in wetlands, when these environments could be converted to uses more directly beneficial to humans as farmland or as land for new housing, marinas, or golf courses. Biodiversity, however, has its own direct benefits for us because different organisms make contributions to:

> *medicine, agriculture, and a variety of sciences. Agronomists continuously refine existing crops, or respond to changing weather patterns or diseases, through worldwide searches for new organisms and undiscovered, genetically distinct populations of well-known species. Drug companies engage in searches for promising new medicines in large part by testing diverse plant or animal products. As biological engineering technologies improve, the "genetic library" represented by wild species will only increase in value to humans. Biological diversity also contributes to maintaining the fundamental ecological processes of the planet.[2]*

Even wetlands that are rarely wet serve as the prime habitat for a vast array of plant and animal life. The riparian wetlands of the American Southwest flank dry washes—streams and rivers that are dry most of the year, except during snowmelt and heavy rains. These areas make up only 1 percent of the land in Arizona, yet they are home to more than half of the plant and animal species recorded in that state.[3]

ENDANGERED SPECIES

Many plants and animals currently classified as threatened or endangered are on that list mainly because their preferred habitat has already suffered severe losses. Wetlands are home to about one-third of such species in the United States. Even with federal and state laws to protect them, sources estimate we are still

An anhinga and a Florida red-bellied turtle in the Everglades. Wetlands provide a safe haven for a wide variety of species.

losing between 300,000 and 500,000 acres (121,500 and 202,500 hectares) of wetlands each year. How will endangered species be able to survive if their habitat shrinks annually?

Perhaps the future agricultural or medicinal value of any one such species is a long shot, but it's impossible to foresee which endangered plant or animal might be expendable. As one writer observed, "Who could have predicted we'd find penicillin in a crummy mold?"[4] In addition, within the fragile wetland ecosystem, a loss at one level may have wider reverberations. The extinction of a species in one particular swamp both increases its risk of disappearing altogether and has an impact on its natural predators, who must find alternate species to feed upon. In addition, the loss of biodiversity can diminish the enjoyment and appreciation humans get from nature.

WATERFOWL

As mentioned above, ducks, geese, and grebes may rest, feed, or nest in wetlands. In fact, such waterfowl "require a variety of different wetland types for wintering, for resting during migration, and for breeding. Many of these wetlands are wet only in the winter or for short periods in which waterfowl use them."[5]

As waterfowl migrate south each autumn, they fly along certain courses that generations of birds have followed before. These air routes are called flyways; there are four of them in North America—the Atlantic, the Mississippi, the Central, and the Pacific. (It's those birds along the Mississippi and Central flyways that breed in the prairie pothole region.) When migrating thousands of miles, waterfowl visit wetlands in the South for wintering, in the North for breeding, and in between for resting along the way.

While other functions of wetlands are as important

as providing habitat for waterfowl, no other purpose is so well known and universally acknowledged. Naturalists have been conducting bird censuses for years. Studies have shown that as wetland areas decrease, bird populations suffer a corresponding drop. The presence of waterfowl and other birds enhances the recreational value of wetlands, as we shall see.

FISHES

Coastal wetlands are tremendously important to commercial fishing, which is a major business in America. A high percentage of the species caught for consumption use these areas as breeding, rearing, or feeding grounds.

In addition, inland freshwater wetlands play an indirect role that aids the health of the fishing industry. These upstream wetlands prevent floods and filter out pollutants, thus enhancing and protecting the environment of the estuaries into which their water eventually flows. Those estuaries, in turn, shelter fish and shellfish during parts of their lives. Scientists have shown, for example, that 98 percent of the commercial fish caught in the Gulf of Mexico and 94 percent of those caught in the southeast Atlantic use estuaries at some point.[6] When estuaries and coastal wetlands are reduced or polluted, fish populations suffer.

Freshwater fish also frequent wetlands, often requiring their shallow waters for breeding and feeding or as a refuge from predators.

FLOOD CONTROL

As the floods in the summer of 1993 in the upper Mississippi River basin attest, the combination of loss of life, loss of property, and economic hardships caused by flooding can be a major problem. The role of wetlands in reducing the potential damage of severe floods is well established. Two different studies have indicated that watersheds with a significant portion of wetlands (15 percent in one study, 30 percent in the other) have flood peaks that are 60 percent lower than those in watersheds with little or no wetlands.[7] Some experts also believe that the increase in flood damage over the last twenty-five years can be traced at least partly to the loss of wetlands.

All natural landscapes have some ability to absorb rainfall, but wetlands almost seem designed for that purpose. The inherent facility of temporary or seasonal wetlands to act as natural sponges is particularly important. For instance, while the swamps found alongside western rivers like Arizona's Verde River are arid most of the year, they are often the only buffer zone against flash floods.

When floodwaters enter a wetland, they lose speed. The wetland acts like a reservoir, releasing the water to flow downstream gradually over the next few hours, days, or weeks. The sediment the floodwater has carried with it settles in slower water—in this way, erosion decreases and the soils of the wetland are further enriched.

When we develop wetlands for nonagricultural use, we construct not only homes, shopping centers, or factories but also the necessary infrastructure—particularly parking lots and roads—to support the buildings. All this development covers up land that could be absorbing heavy rainfall, thus increasing runoff and the likelihood of floods. Sometimes in urban and suburban areas, expensive storm-sewer systems need to be built to duplicate the lost natural ability of wetlands to control flooding.

In addition, some of the waters trapped in wetlands during floods filter down through the soil to the aquifer, the underlying groundwater system. Because many communities in the United States get their drinking water from aquifers, the replenishment wetlands provide is vitally important.

POLLUTION CONTROL

All aquatic ecosystems have some ability to clean themselves naturally. Dilution serves an important function here, as do the bacteria and algae in the water that break down organic matter.

With the increased use of fertilizers in this century has come a massive increase in the amount of nitrogen and phosphorus in runoff from agricultural lands into our nation's rivers. Nutrients such as these become pollutants once they enter an aquatic system. They can contribute to algae blooms and cause fish populations to die off; they can also contaminate the water table. Meanwhile, massive amounts of sediment from erosion can inhibit fish spawning.

Wetlands can directly absorb some of these nutrients, and another portion is trapped in the sediment that wetlands catch, to be used by wetland plants later. By recycling nutrients and filtering sediment, wetlands are prime natural cleaning systems. What's more, pilot projects have shown that wetlands can effectively filter and reduce pollutants, including sewage effluent (see pages 115–19).

When wetlands are left undisturbed, their role in controlling water pollution is the cheapest solution available. When these areas are developed, however, water pollution in the surrounding region can shoot up. For instance, higher levels of nitrogen and phosphorus in the aquifer affect the quality of drinking water drawn up to the surface by private and municipal wells. It may then be necessary to build expensive treatment facilities.

In addition to their role in controlling water pollution, wetlands have a positive effect on air quality as well. These habitats lock up large amounts of carbon that might otherwise enter the earth's atmosphere in the form of carbon dioxide, which has been identified as one of the principal causes of global warming.[8]

RECREATION AND OTHER USES

Even though family picnics rarely take place in the middle of swamps, wetlands are still crucial in providing recreational opportunities for Americans. Nature lovers and bird watchers visit swamps, marshes, and bogs. Those who enjoy fishing or hunting often pursue those activities there. Wetlands draw tourists eager to explore a habitat very different from those in which they pass most of their lives.

Two other things about wetlands and the recreation industry need to be emphasized. First, fishing in open bodies of water and hunting in uplands environments often are highly dependent on the continued existence, and health, of wetlands, because a majority of the fish and waterfowl spend part of their life cycles there.

Second, recreation can be as important to the nation's economy as it is to our individual well-being. A 1980 study estimated that more than $41 billion was spent that year on fish- and wildlife-related recreation—most of which was based on wetland resources.[9] Tourism and recreation provide jobs for many people, contributing to the economic health of many areas in North America.

Some of the other values that wetlands have are less direct, in that they serve to benefit other ecosystems. Those other ecosystems are habitats that in turn provide benefits for humans. For example, we've seen how the commercial fishing industry, which harvests fish and shellfish out of oceans, seas, and bays, would

Canoers get a chance to contemplate the wonders of the Okefenokee Swamp.

shrink drastically were coastal wetlands not available as spawning, nursing, or feeding areas.

Similarly, the continued existence of wetlands supports and enhances the natural aspects of nearby lakes, forests, and parks—most prominently by being a crucial habitat for many bird and fish species that spend other parts of their life cycles elsewhere.

Wetlands, especially coastal ones, play an important role in soil conservation. Coastal wetlands control erosion through reducing wind action and through cushioning the blows of high tides (which also protects populated uplands).

Finally, only 2 percent of all existing plant species have been tested for possible medicinal value. Sources estimate that one-quarter to one-half of all prescription drugs are derived from plants. Since wetlands are home to many threatened and endangered plants—some of which may have a medicinal use that has yet to be discovered—their preservation is vitally important to the future health of humankind.

MEASURING THE VALUE OF WETLANDS

When land developers and environmentalists face off on a particular proposal, economic factors inevitably form part of the debate. Let's say a coastal marsh is a candidate for conversion to a marina in a complex that will include waterfront shops, restaurants, and businesses. Those in favor of the project can point to numerous economic advantages the complex will provide: the jobs that the construction project would create, the jobs the finished development would create, the tax dollars added to the community's coffers, the value of goods and services produced by the businesses that occupy the space, and so on. On the other hand, those opposed to the project must rely on less tangible arguments—for instance, about crucial habitats for threatened species, the dangers of overdevelopment, or the beauty of conserving the piece of land in its natural state. Many of these arguments may not hold weight in influencing local opinion.

This example typifies an enormous problem the environmental movement has faced. It is very difficult to measure, or quantify, the economic value of natural preservation. Conventional analyses do not take into account the economic benefits, both direct and indirect, of clean air and clean water. Nor do they consider the costs of depleting natural resources, degrading soils, or otherwise encroaching on the natural heritage future generations will inherit.

The costs and benefits of environmental regulation and preservation are also hard to measure. Assigning a dollar value to the preservation of a threatened species or ecosystem is no easy task. The ratio of costs to benefits may change from the short term (where the loss of jobs may overshadow all other factors, for example) to the long term (benefits that emerge decades later can seem remote and intangible now).

Finally, costs and benefits are distributed unevenly. Imagine that the marina complex in our example is not built and the land is left in its natural state. The people who own the wetland are the ones who will bear the brunt of the cost, in terms of loss of income. Those who may have had jobs constructing the marina, or working for the businesses that would have located there, also share the burden.

On the other hand, many people might enjoy exploring the pristine wetland if it's turned into a preserve, and even those picnicking in a nearby upland park might derive some benefit from watching birds visiting from the wetland. Still, very few, if any, of these people will think in terms of assigning a specific monetary value to the time spent in such recreational activities. Whatever the overall benefit of maintaining the land as a preserve (which might actually be higher than the monetary benefits of development), it would be spread over a far greater population and a much longer time.

Social, political, and economic considerations play a major part in any discussion of the merits of preserving or developing a wetland or other wild area. In the past, economic analyses have almost always supported development. With the appearance of the new science of environmental economics, this might soon change.

3

THE FLORA AND FAUNA
OF WETLANDS

Such rich and diverse ecosystems as wetlands are home to countless plants and animals. Let's look at some of the more interesting species.

PLANTS

We have already seen how scientists classify plants in marshes as emergents, aquatics, or submergents. In addition, plants can be classified by how often they appear in wetlands. Obligate species (short for "obligatory wetland species") almost always grow in wetlands. Populations of facultative-wetland species are found primarily in wetlands. Facultative species grow equally in wetlands and uplands, while facultative-upland species usually grow in uplands but are occasionally found in wetlands. These classifications are an important tool in identifying wetlands and delineating their boundaries: next to the kind of soil in the area, the distribution of these various kinds of plants is the most important determinant of wetland status.

To survive in wetlands, plants must adapt to specific conditions. The soil may be saturated temporarily, seasonally, or even permanently. This saturation means that oxygen is less readily available to the plant (plants generally take in oxygen through their root systems, and oxygen diffuses much more slowly in water than in air). Two-thirds of the plant species in North America cannot exist in wetlands.

Here are some of the most representative of the plants that have made adaptations that enable them to survive in wetlands:

Bald Cypress ▪ The tall, majestic bald cypress (*Taxodium distichum*), the characteristic tree of southern cypress swamps, is actually a member of the redwood family and is not a true cypress. Its spreading branches, with their needlelike leaves, are often draped with Spanish moss. An even more distinctive feature of the bald cypress is its "knees," the buttressing roots that protrude out of the water. These knoblike extensions of the root system have two purposes. First, they provide additional support for the tree as it sits in wet, unfirm soil. Second, the buttresses are an additional place for the roots to draw in gases, especially when high water prevents the "regular" roots from doing so. (With the soil in swamps saturated, the root system can obtain only a small portion of the oxygen the tree needs.)

Like the tamarack, the bald cypress is a tree that is both coniferous and deciduous: it bears cones, yet it drops its leaves each autumn. Long valued for its durable lumber, the tree has been heavily logged, and large stands of it are now found only in preserves, such as the Big Cypress National Preserve in Florida. As the bald cypress ages, it hollows out inside; the tree survives, but it is no longer considered desirable lumber.

The closely related pond cypress is a smaller tree found in less flooded areas. Pond cypresses are often grouped in domes, slightly elevated areas alongside

The knees of the bald cypress tree not only provide support but also draw in needed gases from the atmosphere.

water-filled depressions. Several theories have been proposed to explain these formations, but scientists remain unsure about how they developed.

Bladderwort ▪ Swollen bladderwort (*Utricularia inflata*) is a carnivorous emergent related to the snapdragon. Oval bladders with trigger hairs are attached to some of the plant's submerged leaves. If swimming prey, such as a tiny crustacean, touches a trigger hair, a doorlike flap of tissue swings open, the bladder suddenly expands, and the prey is sucked inside. Enzymes gradually decompose the organism so that the plant can obtain nitrogen and other nutrients. Swollen bladderwort is especially common in southern bottomland swamps; its relative, the horned bladderwort (*U. cornuta*), favors bogs and uplands.

Bromeliads ▪ Found in coastal swamps in subtropical and tropical regions of the Americas, bromeliads are a family of rootless plants related to the pineapple. They live on tree trunks and among the topmost leaves of trees. They're classified not as parasites but as epiphytes—plants that take moisture and nutrients from the air and rain. Lacking a root system, they must be highly efficient and store water and nutrients in their tightly packed leaves for later use. The most common bromeliads in the United States are wild pine (*Tillandsia fasciculata*), which favors cypress trees, and Spanish moss (*T. usneoides*), which, being an epiphyte, is not a true moss.

Cattails ▪ The cattail (*Typha*) is one of the plants people most frequently associate with marshes. There are ten species of cattails in the world, three of which are native to the United States. Cattails, which can't survive in water deeper than 3 feet (1 m), have underground stems known as rhizomes. Because these rhizomes spread so rapidly, cattails are usually found in dense colonies, with little other vegetation among them. While the rootstock is edible—it was indeed eaten by Native Americans and early colonists—few wetlands animals other than the muskrat feed on the cattail.

Cranberry ■ While found as far south as North Carolina and as far west as Illinois and Minnesota, the cranberry (*Vaccinium macrocarpon*) is commonly associated with New England. The slender, creeping vine-like plant with petite leathery evergreen leaves has pinkish white flowers that are visible in Sphagnum bogs in early summer.

Prized for its dark red berries, the cranberry is one of the few crop plants indigenous to the United States. When it was first cultivated commercially, at the end of the nineteenth century, farmers made minor adjustments to a bog's natural ecology to enhance its growth. For example, they weeded out native species such as the bog aster, which often crowd the less aggressive cranberry, or they adjusted the water level. These days, it's more likely the cranberry bog has been cleared, leveled, drained, and then reflooded in preparation for cranberry monoculture.[1]

Since the berries themselves are extremely tart, they are often sweetened after harvesting, before they reach the Thanksgiving table.

Jack-in-the-pulpit ■ A wildflower that is abundant in swamps in the eastern half of the United States, jack-in-the-pulpit (*Arisaema triphyllum*) can bloom as early as April. Out of a striped, arching leaf called a spathe, there emerges a spike, or spadix, with tiny flowers. As the spathe continues to grow, it arches over the spike, resembling a preacher in a pulpit and giving the plant its name.

Jack-in-the-pulpit is also notable for its ability to change from male to female. Many plants begin life as males but then bear both male and female flowers, and finally end their days with only female flowers. Since it takes more energy for female plants to produce fruit than for male plants to produce pollen, experiments suggest that this transformative ability helps the plant survive in darker or nutrient-poor habitats.[2]

If the bulblike section of the roots, or corm, is eaten raw, it will severely burn the mouth. However, Native Americans cooked the corm to eliminate this peppery effect; they also combined the corm with the female plant's red fruit to create a natural insecticide.

Leatherleaf ▪ A member of the heath family, leatherleaf (*Chamaedaphne calyculata*) is one of the few plants that can thrive in bogs. In fact, its presence is important for the development of a healthy bog. Once a leatherleaf colonizes floating mats of Sphagnum moss, any branch can root easily at its node. In this way, leatherleaf rapidly forms large colonies and the many intertwined woody roots that result strengthen the mat. As dense patches of leatherleaf continue to spread, other plants move in as well, finding it easier to gain a footing on the reinforced mat.

Other heaths include bog tea (*Ledum*), bog rosemary (*Andromeda*), and bog laurel (*Kalmia*). All these groups of heaths have made adaptations in order to survive in bogs. They generally have thick, leathery, elliptically shaped leaves, which prevent water loss and wilting. Interestingly, similar adaptations are seen in desert plants, and for the same reason—the scarcity of water. Here in the bog the plentiful water underneath the floating mat is too acidic to be of much use, so plants make the same kind of adaptations to reduce evaporation loss that they make in arid habitats.

Heaths and orchids also thrive in bogs because of

Southern swamps are home to varieties of handsome flowers, including an iris (left) and a pitcher plant.

their symbiotic relationship with mycorrhizae, acid-loving soil fungi. Mycorrhizae live in the orchid's roots and provide it with a ready source of nutrients. Orchids flourish in bogs partly because they're often the only undisturbed habitat left for their acid-loving guests. At least fourteen species of orchids have been recorded in a Sphagnum moss mat of 1 acre (0.4 hectare).

Mangroves ▪ There are several different groups of plants called mangroves, which are not all that closely related. The red mangrove (*Rhizophora mangle*) typically establishes itself first in a mangrove swamp. Red mangrove has a unique germination: the fruit grows roots before it falls from the tree, so it's ready to root when it drops onto the salty swamp bottom, where the soil is too salty for seeds to germinate. In areas where currents and waves are quiet, the mangrove also has the ability to spread to shallow tidal waters; after a period of time, these shallow waters can be converted to higher, drier land as the red mangrove traps silt around itself and new soil is gradually added.[3]

In Florida, two other species join the red mangrove to form three distinct zones in mangrove swamps. Black mangrove (*Avicennia germinans*) grows on the inland side of the red mangrove. Among the adaptations to its salty environment are aerial roots (pneumatophores), which can be a foot long. These draw in gases that the regular roots cannot get from the dense, decaying mud the plant sits in. White mangrove (*Laguncularia racemosa*) sits on elevated ground above the high-tide mark, on the inland side of the black mangrove. Black mangrove and, to a lesser extent, white mangrove, grow farther north in Florida, but none of these trees can exist north of subtropical areas. The only places they are found in the United States outside Florida are Louisiana (black) and Hawaii (red).

Pitcher Plant ▪ The northern pitcher plant (*Sarracenia purpurea*) roots in the quaking vegetative mat of bogs rather than in soil. It has adapted a unique way to compensate for the nutrient-poor ecosystem it frequents—it eats insects. Its pitcher-shaped leaves collect water, thus attracting thirsty insects. At the lip of the pitcher, slippery bristlelike hairs point downward, permitting the insect to slide into the water. Once there, it cannot climb back up the slippery hairs and eventually drowns. The pitcher plant secretes enzymes to decompose its prey, and nutrients are then absorbed by the leaf.

Other species of the pitcher found in swamps and marshes in the South and the West secrete a nectar that lures insects into the deadly goblets.

Red Maple ▪ The red maple tree (*Acer rubrum*) is found widely east of the Mississippi River, but it is particularly dominant in northern swamps. In the spring, new reddish twigs sprout distinctive globular buds, which then burst into red and yellow flowers, even before the leaves are out. The fruits also mature in the spring, and their seeds are easily dispersed by the wind, helping this handsome shade tree spread farther.

Sphagnum Moss ▪ There are more than 300 species of Sphagnum moss. Because the acidic nature of bogs inhibits the growth of bacteria and other microorganisms, Sphagnum moss is nearly a sterile medium. And because it can absorb more than 100 times its weight in water, it's used by gardeners to keep plants moist during shipping, and when dried, to help retain moisture in poor soil. There are also records of

54

The pitcher plant's distinctively shaped leaves entice and trap insects so that the plant can eat them.

its being used to dress soldiers' wounds during the Russo-Japanese War of 1904–1905.

Sundews ▪ Another carnivorous plant, the round-leaved sundew (*Drosera rotundifolia*), has striking white flowers that sit atop a leafless stalk. At its base the stalk is surrounded by a rosette, a circular cluster of reddish green leaves. This is the plant's means of catching insects. These leaves are covered with sticky glandular hairs, or tentacles, that exude drops of a powerful adhesive. Drawn to the sundew by its coloration and by what appear to be drops of dew on the ends of these hairs, the insect becomes stuck on a tentacle. In unison, neighboring tentacles lean over to quickly smother the prey. Death follows in as little as fifteen minutes, after which decomposition and digestion can take several weeks.

The round-leaved sundew is common in bogs; cousins like the thread-leaved and spatula-leaved sundews can be found in other wetlands.

Touch-me-not ▪ The preferred habitat of the spotted touch-me-not, also called the jewelweed (*Impatiens capensis*), is the northern swamp. Its name derives from its fruit capsule, which explodes at the slightest touch, dispersing the seed. Native Americans valued the touch-me-not for medicinal purposes—for instance, juice from its stem was used to treat poison ivy—and modern science has confirmed the plant's fungicidal quality.

Venus's-flytrap. ▪ Venus's-flytrap (*Dionaea muscipula*) is not only the most famous but also the most efficient of all the plants that have adapted to wetland conditions by becoming insectivorous. It is found almost exclusively in marshes in North and South Carolina, and in both states it's currently an endangered species.

Insects are drawn to the plant by the sweet nectar it exudes. But as an insect lands on a leaf, it invariably brushes one of the trigger hairs on the leaf's circumference, which causes the hinged leaf to close within three seconds. While the intruder is held inside, the trap secretes a digestive enzyme. The digestive process takes several days, after which the leaf reopens.

Water Lilies ▪ The tuber of water lilies, which are found in bogs and marshes, is nutrient-filled and has been used for food by Native Americans. The flowers and leaves of the fragrant water lily (*Nymphaea odorata*), one of the most widespread white water lilies, float on the water. On most land plants, the stomata—the minuscule openings on the surface of the leaf through which carbon dioxide and other gases enter and leave the plant—are on the lower surface, facing the ground. Water lilies have their stomata on the upper, shiny surface—a classic example of the kind of adaptation wetlands plants make.

White Cedar ▪ The Atlantic white cedar (*Chamaecyparis thyoides*) is found in swamps and on the edges of bogs from Cape Cod south. It's a light-loving evergreen that finds it hard to compete with the more shade-tolerant red maple. However, where fire has cleared out a wetland, white cedar will thrive (as long as seeds are present), and it's the dominant species in some swamps, such as those in New Jersey's Wawayanda State Park. The durable wood of the white cedar has been popular since colonial times.

BIRDS

Birds flourish in wetlands, and swamps and marshes are prime spots for bird-watching. (Most of the birds seen in bogs are visitors from surrounding uplands.) Waterfowl are especially partial to marshes, but their

The beautiful water lily is a typical wetland plant.

populations are shrinking these days. Studies have shown that about 66 million ducks migrate annually along the four North American flyways, breeding in Canada and the northern United States and wintering in the South. But that figure is less than half the count of the 1940s. Ecologists believe the major reason for the decrease in waterfowl population is the loss of wetland habitats. In fact, ducks feel that loss at both ends of their migratory cycle. Many breeding grounds in the prairie potholes of the upper Midwest and Canada have been drained for agricultural use, while in southern latitudes, wetlands in areas like California's Central Valley and the Mississippi Delta have been converted into farmlands or developed for housing, offices, or malls. In Louisiana, areas where birds once wintered have been dredged into canals to facilitate oil and gas exploration.[4]

DUCKS

All kinds of marshes are frequented by ducks, who use different habitats throughout the year. They winter in southern wetlands, stop at others for rest and feeding during spring and fall migrations, and use northern wetlands—particularly the prairie potholes of the upper Midwest and Canada—to breed.

When ducks head north in late winter, they rest at seasonal wetlands, where the thaw has increased water runoff to the point where it collects in hollows and basins. Once they arrive at their northern, summer home, some of the wetlands they go to first are temporary or seasonal ones. In both cases, the habitat is a large producer of foods such as insects, worms, crustaceans, and small amphibians.

The first ducks—primarily mallards, pintails, and canvasbacks—arrive at prairie potholes in late March or early April. Some dozen other species, including gadwalls, American wigeons, northern shovelers,

The female mallard's coloring acts as camouflage so that it can nest safely in the high grasses of a marsh.

green-winged teals, lesser scaup, and redheads, follow shortly thereafter.

For ducks to breed successfully, the potholes should feature adequate foods and only a limited number of predators. There are four types of prairie pothole—temporary, seasonal, semipermanent, and permanent—and each one has its value in promoting duck breeding. Dabblers (see later) in particular need a complex of potholes of various sizes in order to breed successfully. They tend to arrive north when thawing is still under way, earlier than the diving ducks do. Therefore, dabblers feed at temporary potholes, because the water level at permanent and semipermanent potholes is at its highest level of the year, too deep for them to feed. Dabblers later build nests in the vegetation on the edges of other nearby potholes, or sometimes in surrounding uplands.

An area with many smaller wetlands is often a better breeding ground for ducks than an ecosystem based around one large wetland. This is because ducks need the sheltered cover that vegetation around the shoreline provides, and small, separate wetlands have more shoreline than a single wetland of the same total size. In addition, waterfowl need some isolation from other birds in order to breed, and small, temporary, or seasonal wetlands close to permanent ones often provide privacy. Nevertheless, while these marshes are the ideal habitat for breeding, predators such as mink, foxes, and raccoons will take eggs, and small ducklings fall prey to snakes, snapping turtles, and hawks.

In the fall, the migration patterns are reversed and the birds head south, again stopping at wetlands such as the Valentine National Wildlife Refuge in Nebraska along the way. Among the places ducks winter are the lower Mississippi floodplain, where almost a third of the mallards in the United States spend the colder months in bottomland hardwood swamps, and the freshwater coastal ponds of south Texas, temporary wetlands that are host to more than half of the wintering redhead ducks of North America and a significant number of pintails as well.

Ducks can be classified as dabblers or as diving ducks. Dabblers search for their food standing in shallow water, often tipping up their tails as they hunt for aquatic plants or animals at or near the pond or wetland bottom. The wigeon, northern shoveler, pintail, mallard, and gadwall are typical dabblers. Diving ducks frequent deeper marshes, as well as lakes and ponds; as the name indicates, they dive underwater to find food. Their legs are placed farther back on their bodies than those of dabblers, increasing their agility under the surface. Among the divers are the canvasback, redhead, ruddy duck, and lesser scaup.

The North American ducks that thrive in marshes are members of the genera *Anas, Aythya,* and *Oxyura.* The relatively tame mallard (*Anas platyrhynchos*) is the most populous species of North American duck. With its distinctive green head and white neck band, the male mallard is very recognizable (the males of many duck species have brighter colors than the females). The fast-flying green-winged teal (*A. crecca*) is a hardy species that is often the last to go south for the winter; it's quite popular as a game bird. The northern shoveler (*A. clypeata*) is a dabbler named for its long black bill, which comes in handy for feeding on minute aquatic animals and aquatic plants. Another dabbler, the American wigeon (*Anas americana*), often snatches food away from diving birds as they resurface.

Two divers have suffered significant population losses in recent years and are considered threatened. The canvasback (*Aythya valisineria*) has a whitish body and an unusual sloping forehead, which distinguishes it from the redhead (*Aythya americana*). The latter bird, which has a gray body, feeds mostly at night, resting on the water surface by day. A third diver, the ruddy duck (*Oxyura jamaicensis*), gets its name from the male's distinctive chestnut body; these ducks rarely fly, preferring to escape predators by diving or by hiding themselves in vegetation on the marsh edge.

At least two species, the wood duck and the black duck, break the mold by preferring swamp over marshes. Both sexes of the American black duck (*Anas rubripes*) are actually more brown or tan. Unlike the friendly mallard, with whom it frequently interbreeds, the black duck is shy, usually concealing its brood in the thick swamp cover. By contrast, the wood duck (*Aix sponsa*) prefers to nest near swamps in hollow trees. Recently, as humans have removed old timber and these habitats shrink, nest boxes have been substituted for the wood duck to use, with some success. The drakes, or male ducks, desert the female shortly before the eggs hatch. The drakes then leave breeding areas to gather in groups in more secluded water habitats; they molt there, losing all their flight feathers as well, so they are unable to fly for weeks until new plumage grows in.[5]

Even though the species discussed above (and many others) favor wetlands, they can often be spotted at ponds and lakes, rivers and streams, especially during migratory periods. Many other ducks, such as mergansers, prefer open water and surrounding riverbanks to wetlands.

OTHER WATERFOWL

The Canada goose (*Branta canadensis*) is another marsh-loving bird. It's also common in urban and suburban parks and reservoirs. Familiar because of the V-shaped flight pattern of the flocks during migration, the Canada goose is found throughout the North American continent. Other geese have a much more

The Canada goose is a familiar sight in wetlands throughout North America.

limited range. The snow goose *(Chen caerulescens)*, for example, nests in Siberia, Alaska, and the arctic tundra of Canada but winters in selected marshes in California, Louisiana's gulf coast, and the shoreline of the mid-Atlantic states.

Grebes are expert divers who often are drawn to marshes, where they can breed privately in concealing vegetation. They build floating nests on rafts they've constructed from rushes and other marsh plants. Once the eggs are hatched, grebes carry their young about on their backs. Among the most common are the eared *(Podiceps nigricollis)* and the pied-billed *(Podilymbus podiceps)*.

Other waterfowl, such as loons and swans, favor the open waters of lakes, ponds, and coastal lagoons.

OTHER WETLAND BIRDS

Wetlands are the favored habitat of hundreds of kinds of birds. Many more stop there occasionally, whether on a quick trip for food from a nearby upland or on a semiannual migration. Here are just a few of the representative species that make marshes and swamps their homes.

Anhinga ▪ The anhinga *(Anhinga anhinga)* favors southern swamps and the Everglades. Also known as the snakebird (because of how it looks when swimming, with its body submerged and only its head and long snakelike neck visible) and the darter, the anhinga dives underwater to grab its prey. Frogs' eggs, aquatic insects, and fish are favorite foods for this black-coated diver. Like its relative the cormorant, anhingas don't have the oil glands most birds use for preening their feathers. Therefore, after being in the water, the anhinga must perch with its wings open to dry.

Bitterns ▪ Bitterns are members of the heron family. The medium-size American bittern (*Botaurus lentiginosus*) has a wide range, covering almost all of the continental United States and large portions of Canada. While other herons generally fly away when disturbed, this brownish bird points its neck upward and freezes—except to sway a little in the wind—in a remarkably successful attempt to blend with surrounding waving reeds. The tiniest member of the heron group, the least bittern (*Ixobrychus exilis*) is a secretive bird that lives in marshes in the eastern half of the United States.

Blackbirds ▪ With a range covering most of the North American continent, the red-winged blackbird (*Agelaius phoeniceus*) has a rich, musical call that birdwatchers love. The male is easily recognizable by the red shoulder patches on its otherwise black body; the females are dark brown. When a pair of birds mate, they build a nest in reeds or shrubs not too far off the ground. For much of the year, redwings congregate in huge flocks called ranks, but during the summer they hide in vegetation as their flight feathers molt and replacements grow in. While most of their diet consists of insects and the seeds of marsh plants (such as cattail and wild rice), redwings are often reviled for wreaking extensive damage on ripened corn fields late in the summer. Authorities have occasionally stepped in to destroy some birds.

The yellow-headed blackbird (*Xanthocephalus xanthocephalus*) is found mostly in the western half of the country. When both species nest in the same marsh, an interesting behavioral pattern emerges. The redwings generally arrive first, mate, and begin staking out territory, but when the more aggressive yellowheads appear, they claim the best nesting sites among the denser bulrushes and cattails. The redwings are thus pushed out to sites directly on the open water or in nearby uplands that offer less cover.

Egrets ▪ The majestic great egret (*Casmerodius albus*) is the largest of the egrets and has the greatest range as well. During the summer, it can be found as far north as Oregon on the West Coast, Minnesota in the Mississippi River valley, and Massachusetts on the East Coast; it winters in the Southeast and along the Gulf Coast. Both the great and the snowy egret (*Egretta thula*) were endangered after extensive hunting for their fine white plumage, but populations seem to have stabilized now that hunting the birds has been outlawed.

Some egrets employ interesting feeding techniques. The snowy egret sticks one foot in the water as it flies just above a wetland, thus flushing out its prey. The reddish egret (*E. rufescens*), which is found only in Florida mangrove swamps and coastal wetlands in Texas, dashes around with its wings outspread; the shadows its wings cast attract its prey.

Gallinule ▪ The purple gallinule (*Porphyrula martinica*), a member of the rail family, can sometimes be glimpsed walking on lily pads in southern marshes and in the Everglades. When it's not migrating, the bird prefers to walk rather than fly or swim, and its long legs, long neck, and somewhat squat body are adaptations that facilitate moving quickly and easily through dense marsh plants. The brightly colored purple gallinule—it has a yellow-and-red bill, yellow legs, and a greenish back, as well as the bluish purple front shield that provides its name—is remarkably well camouflaged for its wetland habitat. It eats frogs, shellfish, aquatic insects, seeds, and flowers.[6]

Herons ▪ With the widest range of any heron, the great blue heron (*Ardea herodias*) is a very tall wading bird whose long legs, slender neck, and white-and-blue face lend a touch of elegance to any wetland. The great blue can often be seen standing motionless on the edge of a patch of open water, watching for fish or frogs at its feet; most other herons feed in the same way. The great white heron was once thought to be its own species, but this bird, found only in Florida, is actually an all-white variety of the great blue. In some individual habitats in the eastern half of the United States, the small, crow-sized green-backed heron (*Butorides striatus*) is actually more common than the great blue.

Ibis ▪ Another bird related to the heron, the ibis is distinguished by its lengthy curved bill. The two most common species of ibis found in the United States stand about 2 feet (0.6 m) high and have a wingspan of about 3 feet (1 m). The white ibis *(Eudocimus albus)* has a red bill, a white body, and legs that are red during breeding season and slate-colored the rest of the year. The glossy ibis *(Plegadis falcinellus)* has a dark body of chestnut and deep greens, with light brown bill and legs. The white is found in cypress swamps, salt marshes, and mangrove swamps from South Carolina to Texas, while the glossy, which was once quite rare, has now spread up along the Atlantic coast to Maine and has even been sighted around the Great Lakes. Crayfish is a favorite food for both ibises. Another variety of ibis was a sacred bird to the ancient Egyptians.

Rails ▪ Rails are perhaps the most secretive of all the birds that frequent the marshes of North America. They are rarely seen but can sometimes be heard calling at twilight. The source of the expression "thin as a

A great blue heron stands motionless as it searches for food.

rail," they have narrow bodies adapted to easing through dense marsh vegetation. Rails range in height from 6 (the yellow rail, or *Coturnicops noveboracensis*) to 18 inches (the king rail, *Rallus elegans*). Most species are found in freshwater marshes, but the clapper rail (*R. longirostris*) favors coastal saltwater marshes. The sora (*Porzana carolina*) is somewhat threatened by the loss of breeding grounds.

Snail Kite ▪ While the snail kite (*Rostrhamus sociabilis*) has a wide range in Central and South America, in this country it's found only in Florida, concentrated in the Everglades. This dark, crow-sized bird has the dubious distinction of being among the first animals officially listed as endangered, in 1966, when its U.S. population was estimated at twenty-five. While it now numbers in the hundreds, the problem persists.

The snail kite feeds almost exclusively on snails of the genus *Pomacea*, which are often called apple snails. The population of apple snails dips precariously in years when water is scarce, and from both natural and artificial causes, the Everglades has suffered from low water supplies. In addition, the apple snail's shell is highly prized by collectors. Faced with an unreliable food supply and a continuing loss of habitat, the snail kite has been hard-pressed to survive.

In addition, it can be an indifferent breeder. It ordinarily nests in shrubs, which provide adequate shelter from predators, but when higher areas get too dry, it will nest in cattails in marshes. But nests built on these flimsy soft-stemmed plants often collapse, and as few as one-third of its eggs hatch. In years when water levels are high (and the apple snail plentiful), either adult may desert the family, going off to mate again and raise a new brood, a pattern that is unique among birds.[7] (See chapter 5 for more on the problems this endangered bird faces.)

Whooping Crane ▪ The tall whooping crane (*Grus americana*) is one endangered species that has been brought back from the brink of extinction. A census in the early 1940s counted only 15 of these long-necked birds in a colony that wintered on the Texas gulf coast and bred in northern Canada. After years of protective management, there are now about 200 in that flock.

While making their 2,600-mile-long migration, whooping cranes stop at many temporary and seasonal wetlands. Their breeding grounds have been pushed farther north over the years because of development—they now spend the summer in Wood Buffalo Natural Park in the Northwest Territories. Whooping cranes, which mate for life, build their elevated nests out of bulrushes, in marshy areas of the refuge.

Scientists have been breeding the bird in captivity, hoping eventually to reintroduce them into the wild in other areas. In December 1992, they moved a step closer toward that dream, with the release of a dozen birds in a reserve in central Florida. The whoopers there will live with their cousins the sandhill cranes (*Grus canadensis*). A slightly smaller species, the sandhill has never been endangered, partly because many sandhills breed (after a spectacular mating dance) far to the north in the remote Canadian Arctic.

Wood Stork ▪ With its 5½-foot (1.7-m) wingspan and its white body, the wood stork (*Mycteria americana*) cuts an impressive figure. Especially in Florida, where they're more common, wood storks are also known as flintheads because of their gray featherless heads and necks. Although it has a slightly wider range in the United States than the snail kite, it, too, is an endangered species. While it once nested in massive rookeries containing hundreds of pairs of birds, there are now fewer than 1,000 wood storks left in the wild.

The wood stork has a somewhat inefficient method of feeding—it moves through shallow waters with its open beak underwater, searching for fish and small amphibians. When it finds something, it closes its mouth and swallows the prey. This requires a dense concentration of fish populations in shallow marsh waters. The loss of wetlands on the edges of the Everglades has cut fish production, and human "management" of the water in south Florida has created other problems. Sometimes water levels are too high, so that fish populations don't get concentrated as the wood stork requires; the wood stork will even delay breeding until water levels fall. (See chapter 5 for more of the problems this endangered bird faces.)

BIRDS IN NORTHERN SWAMPS

While northern swamps are full of birds, too, there are fewer "representative" species. Birds visit from surrounding uplands for food, or they rest there during migrations. Those that do live in swamps often choose them rather than uplands only because the preponderance of trees provides a secure habitat. Species that favor swamps do so because, as one guidebook puts it, "these areas contain niches that fulfill their requirements. Birds choose nesting sites not because specific species of vegetation are present; instead the choice is based on the structure of the plant cover."[8] For instance, the common yellowthroat (Geothlypis trichas) prefers to nest in low shrubs near the ground; the Canada warbler (Wilsonia canadensis) often nests directly on the ground; the northern waterthrush (*Seiurus noveboracensis*) picks old stumps near water; and the catbird (*Dumetella carolinensis*) gravitates toward shrubby thickets.

MAMMALS

Many kinds of mammals use wetlands during some portion of the year, visiting from surrounding uplands. Among those that frequent wetlands more regularly are the following:

Beaver ▪ Because of its desirable pelt, the beaver (*Castor canadensis*) was once hunted nearly to extinction in both North America and Europe. Enjoying some protection today, this large rodent now has a stable population and is found throughout the continent.

Beavers are very well known for their carefully engineered dams, made of precisely stacked sticks, mud, and stone. The dam incorporates a lodge that can be reached only through an underwater entrance. By building these dams and changing the pattern of water flow, beavers have a profound effect on wetland ecology. For instance, the damming of a small stream can cause the inundation of nearby swamps; the higher water level begins a conversion to a marsh or even a pond. On the other hand, after a period of years, food in this habitat may run out and beavers will move elsewhere. When the animals are no longer around to maintain the dam, it develops larger and larger leaks, and eventually the water level falls. With less standing water, what was a pond can become a marsh, and what was a marsh can become a forested swamp or a wet meadow.

The beaver has several adaptations that enable it to

Beaver dams alter the water flow, here creating a large pond.

thrive in its chosen environment. Its thick fur is provided with natural oils that have insulating and waterproofing qualities. Valves in its ears and snout close tight when it enters the water; these, as well as webbed hind feet and a paddlelike tail, aid in swimming. The beaver is also distinguished by its large incisors; these teeth are worn down by gnawing and felling trees, but they grow continually. While the larger sections of the downed trees are used for building or repairing, the bark and the smaller twigs and branches form the basis of the beaver's diet.

Black Bear ▪ The black bear (*Ursus americanus*) has a wide range throughout the United States and Canada. In the eastern half of the continent, it prefers bogs and swamps, as well as the Everglades; a 1990 study in Massachusetts found that black bears spent an average of 60 percent of the spring and summer feeding in small forested wetlands. In the western half of North America, they are more often found in upland forests. Even though they are classified as carnivores, the bears eat mostly vegetation. Although primarily nocturnal, they can often be seen foraging at open dumps and can be dangerous once they lose their fear of humans.

The species is endangered in some areas, particularly in Louisiana, where fewer than 100 bears remain (down from an estimated 50,000). The black bear is on the threatened list there principally because of the destruction of its bottomland swamp habitat. It needs large contiguous areas to roam through to gather food, so the fragmentation of wetlands after one tract is developed aggravates the problem.

Mink ▪ Early settlers often hunted and trapped mink for their pelts, but for the past century mink have been bred commercially on farms. In the wild, mink have a range that covers all of North America, except for the arctic regions of Canada and Alaska and the Southwest. A member of the weasel family, the mink *(Mustela vison)* spends much of its time in water. It nests in hollow logs, among rocks, and in abandoned muskrat lodges and beaver dens. This carnivore eats freshwater clams, mice, fish, and birds, but its favorite food is the muskrat. The mink kills by biting its prey in the neck, and after feeding it will drag any surplus back to its den to eat later. In turn, mink fall prey to foxes, bobcats, and great horned owls. It gives off a strong odor to delineate its territory and when angered; both sexes are ferocious fighters.

Muskrat ▪ Found throughout most of North America, the muskrat *(Ondatra zibethica)* is another member of the rodent family that exhibits special adaptations for water. Like the beaver, it has waterproof fur, partly webbed hind feet, and a flat tail that can function as a rudder. Muskrats build dome-shaped lodges, great mounds of expertly intertwined plant stems that are often as large as 4 by 6 feet (1.2 by 1.8 m); the nest inside is thus well above the water level of the marsh. As they assemble their homes, muskrats perform a function vital to the health of the wetland ecosystem. The shredded vegetation left behind during construction of the muskrat's lodge is in a form easier for smaller decomposers to attack, setting the detrital food chain into motion.

While muskrats will occasionally feed on mussel and crayfish, they are also voracious eaters of wetland vegetation and are especially partial to cattails, bulrushes, and wild rice. Therefore, when muskrat populations explode, the emergent vegetation is so heavily grazed that "eat-outs" can occur. During an eat-out, all plants in a section of the marsh are consumed and there are suddenly large patches of open water. Ordinarily, overpopulation will bring with it death for the weakest muskrats, as competition for scarce food increases. The fittest survive and the hardy muskrats rebound. (However, the marsh itself will take much longer to recover from the eat-out.) At other times, natural predators, such as the mink, keep muskrat populations stable.

Nutria ▪ The large aquatic rodent called the nutria, or coypu (*Myocastor coypus*), is a sterling example of what biologists call an exotic—a species that is not native to a particular habitat or ecosystem. Nutria were originally imported from Argentina during the first half of the twentieth century by an industrialist who wanted to breed them commercially, as a substitute for beaver fur. However, some escaped into the wild, and nutria have multiplied prodigiously since then, for several reasons. Like many exotics, they started without natural predators; nutria also mature quickly, breed two or three times a year (the female can mate again almost immediately after giving birth), and produce four or five young per litter.

Although they are voracious vegetation grazers, nutria tend to eat only the tops of plants, and thus don't clear out large areas of wetlands the way muskrats do. When disturbed, a nutria will seek refuge in the water, where it can stay submerged for several minutes and where its webbed hind feet come in handy. The female also has her mammary glands on her back, to facilitate suckling while afloat. Concentrated in Louisiana and Texas, the nutria weighs 15 to 20 pounds (6.8 to 9.1 kg) when fully grown. Its distinctive dark orange incisors, which can be glimpsed as it eats, have led to the nickname "orangetooth."

Raccoon ▪ Although widespread in uplands, the raccoon (*Procyon lotor*) also favors swamps. That wetland

Swamps are an ideal habitat for raccoons, offering good nesting places and abundant food.

habitat offers hollow trees, such as bald cypress, in which to nest, as well as crayfish and a variety of other food to feast on. Raccoons will also visit marshes in search of duck and turtle eggs. These omnivores usually forage at night; during the day, they can sometimes be glimpsed stretched out in the sun on the branch of a big tree. Except when breeding or caring for its young, the raccoon prefers to stay by itself; in fact, if its territory is threatened, it can be an excellent fighter. Its range is the southern part of Canada and all of the continental United States, except for portions of the Rocky Mountain states.

White-tailed Deer ▪ Another primarily upland animal, the white-tailed deer (*Odocoileus virginianus*), visits wetlands to graze and will often make forested swamps its home, especially in the winter months. This majestic animal is often sighted throughout southern Canada and every part of the forty-eight states except the Southwest. It's primarily nocturnal and eats a very wide variety of vegetation, including aquatic plants during the summer months. When disturbed, it raises its tail, showing the area underneath that provides its name. Not only does this bright flash of white tell other deer that there is danger nearby, it also gives fawns a way to follow their mother as she flees.

Other mammals, from shrews, voles, and mice to bobcats, foxes, and moose, are dependent on wetlands for food and/or shelter. Among these, two more species deserve a brief mention. The first, the endangered Florida panther, an isolated variety of the mountain lion (*Felis concolor*), is the largest predator in the Southeast; fewer than fifty survive in south Florida. The second, the marsh rabbit (*Sylvilagus palustris*), has evolved an amazing adaptation to help it survive in southern bottomland hardwood swamps and the Everglades. If, as is possible, there is a flood during the breeding season, the female may resorb a developing embryo back into her placenta, delaying birth until conditions are more favorable and thus increasing the chances of newborn rabbits' surviving.

AMPHIBIANS, REPTILES, AND OTHERS

Many species of salamanders and frogs find wetlands a hospitable environment. During their larval stage, these amphibians feed on minute plants and animals, generally in patches of water. When they reach maturity, adult salamanders often eat small animals such as the larger insects and the tinier mice. Bullfrogs have been known to catch and swallow young birds and snakes. Of course, amphibians are often eaten in turn by larger animals.

While numerous species may visit a bog from surrounding marshes, swamps, or uplands, the rare Pine Barrens treefrog (*Hyla andersoni*) is one of the few vertebrates that live there; it's now threatened by the loss of its favored habitats.

Another bog resident is the bog turtle (*Clemmys muhlenbergi*), which is on the protected list in most of the mid-Atlantic states in which it's found. Turtles and other reptiles (snakes, lizards, alligators, and crocodiles) are fairly common in most wetlands. Southern marshes and swamps are home to poisonous snakes such as the cottonmouth (*Agkistrodon piscivorus*) and the timber rattlesnake (*Crotalus horridus*); in the North, the latter species favors remote wooded hills and mountains instead of low-lying wetlands.

The largest reptile in North America is the alligator (*Alligator mississippiensis*), which inhabits the Everglades and swamps and marshes throughout the Southeast. As humans hunted the alligator for its skin, caught it to sell as a pet, and drained its habitat for development, the alligator was threatened with extinction. In recent years it has staged a comeback. Nevertheless, although it has been removed from official endangered species lists in Louisiana, Texas, and Florida, it still enjoys a special protected status.

Intolerant of cold weather, the alligator hibernates during the coolest weeks of the southern winter. In the spring, alligators mate, and the female builds a large mound up to 8 feet high and 3 feet across (2.4 m high and 0.9 m wide) from mud and organic detritus as a nest. She lays 24 to 60 eggs, covering them with more debris. The eggs incubate for about nine weeks, helped by heat from the decaying vegetation, while the female guards the nest. When the hatchlings signal the mother with a distinctive call, she uncovers the nest and helps them out of the shells.[9]

The young eat insects and small crustaceans at first, graduating to fish, frogs, and snakes. Juveniles stay with the mother for one to three years. Adults supplement their diets with small mammals and waterfowl. The alligator is one of the longest-living animals, with a life span as long as fifty-five years.

The alligator has also proved to be a strong link in the survival of vibrant wetlands for two principal reasons, each involving the structures it builds. Once the alligator's nest is abandoned, other wetlands animals use it; in the Everglades especially, abandoned gator nests are refuges for smaller species during flooding.

At the other extreme, during droughts the alligator will dig itself a shallow pool called a gator hole. It will wait out the drought, sitting torpidly in this hole in estivation, an inactive, sluggish state akin to hibernation. The wet mud or what little water remains in this gator hole provides a means of survival for many other wetlands animals as well. They move in alongside the alligator, somehow knowing it's safe during this period to share space with such an imposing predator.

Although no longer in danger of extinction, the mighty alligator continues to receive special protection.

When the rains return, each species goes its own way, and natural predator/prey relationships resume. Meanwhile, the nearby piles of debris, which the alligator had moved to excavate the now abandoned gator hole, become fertile ground for seedlings as marsh plants begin new growth to recover from the drought. Thus, these gator holes are crucial in maintaining habitat diversity during critical dry periods. In fact, in the Everglades, their value is such that the holes themselves are protected by law.

The crocodile (*Crocodylus acutus*) is distinguished from its cousin by a longer, slender snout. Reaching 15 feet (4.6 m) at the most, it's also slightly smaller than the alligator. Crocodiles are found only in south Florida and are still endangered.

Various characteristics of the patches of open water in wetlands inhibit the presence of large populations of fish. The water is generally too shallow and too warm, and it has too little oxygen in it to support most species. Nonetheless, fishes do come to marshes and swamps, especially where these habitats are alongside rivers, streams, and lakes, and thus can serve as places in which to spawn or to find protective cover.

No discussion of wildlife in wetlands can be considered complete without mentioning the most famous resident of swamps and marshes—the common mosquito (*Culex pipiens*). In a way, this insect may be responsible for the preservation of a lot of the world's undeveloped wetlands: since people didn't want to be close to these creatures that bite and draw human blood, they didn't encroach on mosquitoes' favored habitat.

Actually, only the female mosquito bites; the male feeds primarily on plant juices. The female lays her eggs in a raftlike mass that floats on the surface of still water, so the stagnant water of brackish swamps and marshes is prime breeding territory.

The mosquito has evolved in ways that encourage explosively rapid breeding. The eggs take only one to five days to hatch, so the fluctuating water levels of wetlands—including temporary ones, which may only be wet a few weeks annually in years of normal rainfall—are not a threat to successful breeding. In about two weeks, the larvae enter the pupal stage, and the adult emerges soon thereafter, ready to start reproducing as well.

A mosquito bite may be only a minor discomfort, but the insect has also been a carrier of yellow fever and malaria. Efforts to control mosquito populations go back thousands of years (the Romans tried to drain nearby swamps to prevent breeding); these days, larvicides and insecticides are more effective methods than draining, since only minimal amounts of water are needed for breeding. Mosquitoes are a major source of food for wetlands animals, especially when they are in the larval, or wriggler, stage. Thus, while they will continue to be an inconvenience to man, mosquitoes are a crucial link in the wetlands food chain.

4

THE POLITICS OF
PRESERVATION

As Americans become more knowledgeable about wetlands and their importance, various segments of our society have called for a halt to further loss of wetlands. The most conservative estimate suggests that today 300,000 acres (121,500 hectares) a year of wetlands are drained, dredged, filled in, or otherwise altered by humans (more than $1\frac{1}{4}$ square miles [3.25 sq km] every day). The vast majority of these lost acres are drained by farmers for agricultural use. While wetlands now enjoy a significant amount of protection under federal, state, and local laws, their value remains a point of contention for many, and thus there are continual efforts to repeal laws, circumvent their provisions, or undermine their enforcement.

In 1963, Massachusetts became the first state to regulate wetlands use when its legislature passed a law that extended some jurisdiction over the development of coastal marshes. Since then, at least nineteen other states have adopted wetlands legislation of some kind, and many state programs are stricter than the federal government's.

Nevertheless, because state laws vary so widely across the United States, our discussion of the current relationships of government, politics, and wetlands will focus on the federal level. Examining the history of federal wetlands law, and its enforcement, vividly illustrates the effects of different forces—government, farmers, environmentalists, the public at large, developers, industrialists, and small businesspeople—on what protections American wetlands do have.

THE CLEAN WATER ACT

On the federal level, wetlands protection begins with the 1972 passage of the Clean Water Act. Ironically, no language in that legislation explicitly referred to wetlands. The act was to cover "all waters of the United States," and was seen primarily as a way to control water pollution. In the next few years, administrative decisions and judicial rulings confirmed that wetlands were included within its scope and by 1977 the first federal, executive department order explicitly to protect wetlands was issued.

Section 404 of the Clean Water Act has been the keystone on which federal wetlands protection is based. It requires a permit from the Army Corps of Engineers before wetlands can be filled in; it also governs the deposition of fill or dredged material, so the Corps' authority is also extended over any dredging to facilitate navigation. In reauthorizing the Clean Water Act in 1977, the U.S. Congress added specific sections regarding wetlands, including a call for a nationwide inventory to determine exactly how many acres still survived. The law also mandated that the Environmental Protection Agency (EPA) provide guidelines on wetlands and gave it veto power over any Corps decision on the permitting procedure.

Meanwhile, federal policy emanating from the Soil Conservation Service, an agency of the U.S. Department of Agriculture (USDA), continued to encourage the drainage of wetlands for conversion to agricultural use. While the pace of such subsidized conversion had slowed down from its peak of nearly 3 million acres (1.2 million hectares) annually between 1940 and 1960, it was still considerable. In effect, one branch of the government had begun to protect wetlands, but another branch was still subsidizing their destruction.

Congress tried to rectify this situation in 1985 while enacting a major farm bill. The Food Security Act's so-called Swampbuster provision barred subsidies to farmers who drained wetlands, filled them in, *and* harvested a major cash crop on the converted land. Despite good intentions, however, the Swampbuster provisions didn't really fix anything. For one thing, there were large loopholes. A farmer who refrained from harvesting a commodity crop on newly drained land could still receive a federal subsidy. All wetlands converted to agricultural use before 1985 were exempt as long as they were not reconverted to another use, such as residential development.

In addition, the USDA rarely enforced the Swampbuster provisions. In its first five years, hundreds of landowners were caught violating Swampbuster, but fewer than fifteen lost their federal subsidies. During severe droughts in the late 1980s, the USDA even relaxed the provisions.

On top of all that, it turned out that other federal programs also encouraged wetlands destruction. For instance, one study showed that federal flood-control projects in the Mississippi River valley provided economic incentives that encouraged private landowners to drain, dredge, or fill in swamps.

THE 1989 MANUAL

As federal policy was moving fitfully toward increased protection of wetlands, environmentalists were educating Congress, government agencies, and the public on the value of these habitats. Some consensus was building for stronger conservation programs, and George Bush's 1988 presidential campaign pledge of "no net loss" of wetlands was well received.

Meanwhile, four different federal agencies had jurisdiction over wetlands: the Army Corps of Engineers; the USDA's Soil Conservation Service; the Environmental Protection Agency (EPA); and the Department of the Interior's Fish and Wildlife Service. Each agency had developed its own techniques for identifying and delineating wetlands. For instance, the latest set of Corps guidelines, titled *Corps of Engineers Wetland Delineation Manual*, had been issued in 1987.

Because each agency's guidelines were slightly different, a wetland might have one border by the standards of, say, the Soil Conservation Service, but if the criteria of the Corps of Engineers had been applied, the area marked as wetland might have varied considerably. The four agencies began looking for a way to avoid this kind of conflict.

Without seeking public comment, they issued a common definition of wetlands early in 1989, ten days before George Bush was inaugurated. This definition, published as the *Federal Manual for Identifying and Delineating Jurisdictional Wetlands*, was based on the presence of certain kinds of vegetation and soils and the periodic saturation of the root zone (known as the vegetation, soil, and hydrology criteria, respectively).

The publication of this manual was a critical milestone in federal wetlands policy, especially since it coincided with the inauguration of a president who had pledged that he would protect these areas. Wetlands defenders were encouraged by the prospect of the coordinated definition and enforcement policies that the four federal agencies now promised. Continuing the process established by Section 404 of the Clean

Water Act, under the new guidelines anyone wishing to fill a wetland would still have to apply to the Army Corps of Engineers for a permit.

However, those who objected to the joint guidelines pointed out that, contrary to common practice for new government regulations, the manual had been issued without a call for public comment. Government spokespeople responded that there was no need for public comment, since this manual was merely restating a definition that had existed, in various bits and pieces, throughout the Federal Register for years, going back to the 1972 Clean Water Act.

In the next few months, other objections began to filter in to Washington. Farmers whose properties included temporary wetlands protested when they discovered that they now had to apply for permits to alter these mostly dry areas. Shipping interests in Louisiana wanted to continue to dredge canals through that state's coastal marshes. Oil companies objected to the fact that more of the Alaskan tundra was now protected. Once the four agencies, with the new regulations making federal policy clearer, began to step up enforcement, small landowners also joined the protests.

In no agency was the new tenor of federal wetlands policy more apparent than the Army Corps of Engineers. Because the Corps had a long history of promoting huge public works projects (building levees, dredging canals and channels, and so on), many environmentalists viewed it suspiciously. Its track record in defending wetlands left a lot to be desired: when the Corps had promulgated its own wetlands manual in 1987, nearly a third of the Corps' district offices all but ignored it. But after the publication of the joint definition in 1989, there were signs that the Corps wanted to change. In an interview, Chief of Engineers Lieutenant General Henry Hatch said, "We engineers must look at our work in a broad social and environmental context as well as in technical and short-term economic terms."[1]

In general, as the Army Corps of Engineers reviews applications for permits to alter wetlands, it seeks a balance between any loss of wetlands and economic development. The Corps often suggests ways of minimizing damage to wetlands and comments on mitigation plans, proposals to compensate for the loss of wetland acreage by restoring or creating an equivalent amount of wetland nearby (see chapter 6).

In any event, 97 percent of all requests to fill wetlands have eventually been granted permits. (On rare occasions, the EPA has stepped in to overrule an Army Corps of Engineers permit.) But this high percentage doesn't mean the Corps remained a rubber stamp for development. As conservationists themselves have pointed out, the permit process provides an opportunity for third parties to examine any proposed change in the use of a plot of delineated wetland. Many application reviews have resulted in the developer's making modifications to lessen a plan's negative impact on wetland habitat, and the Corps deserves part of the credit for that.

Meanwhile, many small farmers and a considerable number of owners of small plots of land zoned for residential development were unaware that they needed to apply for a permit; they were justifiably angry when the Army Corps of Engineers came after them and enforced the law. Public anger at the increased protection of wetlands was most widespread in the Chesapeake Bay basin (especially on Maryland's Eastern Shore) and Louisiana, both areas that were full of wetlands. Significantly, the district offices of the Army Corps of Engineers had been somewhat lax in enforcing its 1987 manual, so the new regulatory atmosphere came as quite a surprise.[2]

THE 1991 DRAFT REGULATIONS

All those who had run afoul of the stepped-up pace of wetlands law enforcement began to look to Washington for relief. An industry lobbying group called the National Wetlands Coalition formed; belying its name, it sought to weaken regulations and open up more acreage for commercial development and mineral extraction. As these parties lobbied for relaxed wetlands provisions, they found a welcome audience at two White House offices: the Council on Competitiveness and the Domestic Policy Council.

The Bush administration felt that government regulations often imposed a heavy burden on business, and that complying with these regulations lessened American industry's ability to compete in the worldwide economy and even limited economic growth. As a result, the Council on Competitiveness, chaired by Vice President Dan Quayle, was given the mission of reviewing—and if necessary forestalling—government regulations, especially environmental ones, that put too much of an onus on business. Published reports in the spring of 1991 indicated that the council was working with a wetlands panel formed by the Domestic Policy Council to draft a new federal definition of wetlands, one that would exclude some areas from protection and the permit process.

On August 9, 1991, a new proposal incorporating a redefinition of wetlands was released for public comment and congressional review. An accompanying statement from President Bush said that a new policy was important to "slow and eventually stop the net loss of wetlands. . . . The plan seeks to balance two important objectives: the protection, restoration and creation of wetlands and the need for sustained economic growth and development."[3]

Farmers, developers, home builders, and others

adversely affected by the 1989 guidelines immediately praised the plan. However, environmentalists accused Mr. Bush of backing down from his 1988 campaign promise of "no net loss" of wetlands. The resulting controversy increased awareness of wetlands among the public at large far more than almost two decades of evolving legislation and regulation had.

Therefore, even though these proposals were never executed, examining them in some detail helps us understand why they became such a rallying point for almost all parties concerned about wetlands.

EXCLUDING THE "POTHOLE IN THE BACKYARD"

As we have seen, the 1989 manual defined a wetland through specific vegetation, soil, and hydrology criteria. Two of these three criteria had to be present; the third could be inferred from the others. The hydrology, or wetness, criterion was that water be present at or near the surface for seven consecutive days during the growing season. Any change that involved filling a defined wetland had to go through the permit process.

The centerpiece of the Bush administration's 1991 plan, its proposed redefinition of wetlands, was also its most controversial element. In order to qualify, an area would have to have saturated soil at the surface for twenty-one days in the growing season, or standing water for fifteen consecutive days at other times of the year.

In addition, once a wetland was delineated, it would be ranked as a natural resource. Only those habitats judged to have the highest natural value would receive the fullest protection; those in the lowest of the three categories would be open to development without going through any permit or review process.

Administration spokespeople said the August 1991 plan would ensure continuing protection of "real" wetlands, while rolling back regulations on "borderline" wetlands—what one official termed "potholes in the backyard"—that, they claimed, had not been covered before the 1989 interagency manual.

Developers, builders, and farmers responded to this proposal with cautious enthusiasm. Some were pleased that the government had finally heard their pleas about the ravages of overzealous regulation. They continued to lobby, both before the executive branch and with Congress, for more comprehensive action. Small property owners who had run up against government restrictions on the use of their land were now every bit as involved in this effort as were the giant corporations that had formed the National Wetlands Coalition.

THE ENVIRONMENTALISTS STRIKE BACK

In the environmental community, the Bush administration's new plan was not greeted warmly. In its first reaction to the announcement, the Environmental Defense Fund estimated that these rules would take one-third of the nation's wetlands out from under the protective umbrella of current regulations. The president of the National Wildlife Federation said that the new policy was "a death sentence for millions of acres of this critical American resource."[4]

During the period set aside for hearings and public comment on the proposals, environmentalists proceeded to marshal a considerable amount of support for their objections, particularly from the scientific community. By January 1992, for instance, two prominent organizations published a massive critique of the Bush plan, with input from more than forty scientists.[5]

The revisions in the hydrology, vegetation, and soil criteria used to delineate wetlands were all criticized. They lacked a proven scientific basis, wetlands defenders said. The process of delineating wetlands would also be much more onerous, with requirements for more data and tests that could be performed only by a few highly trained specialists. In sum, the report estimated, if the proposed changes took place, 50 percent of the areas in the lower forty-eight states currently classified as wetlands would no longer meet the definition. The door to development would open for millions of acres.

Because they called for a longer continuous period of saturation, the hydrology requirements came under particular scrutiny. Saturation had to occur during the growing season (itself redefined in such a way that it was effectively shorter) and at the surface instead of at root level. Adopting these standards would mean the exclusion of many wetlands—those that are inundated frequently but never for twenty-one straight days (for instance, marshes and swamps near rivers and streams that receive floodwaters, which then quickly recede—these areas are then dry until the next heavy rain); those that are wet primarily in the winter and early spring, outside of the growing season; those where the water table is often high at root level but rarely at the surface; and those that are dry most of the time but become wet in times of flash floods (especially along rivers in the West).

Some of the vegetation requirements also proved troubling to environmentalists. The 1989 manual acknowledged that facultative and facultative-upland species often appear in wetlands, in some cases even dominating the ecosystem. Therefore, it allowed for an area to be identified as a wetland if hydrology and soil conditions warranted. However, the 1991 plan treated these kinds of plants as neutral, requiring that obligate and facultative-wetland plants predominate. Here again, the rules would exclude many habitats. For instance, in large portions of the Everglades an exotic tree called the melaleuca grows so aggressively that other plants are crowded out. Because the melaleuca was brought to south Florida by landscapers to be planted outside corporate headquarters and in backyards, it's classified as a facultative plant (ironically, it's a wetland plant in its native Australia). Its dominance in portions of America's largest wetland (a problem that 1992's Hurricane Andrew only exacerbated—see page 111) would mean that those areas would no longer meet the vegetation requirements; they would not be considered wetlands under the new rules.

The objections raised to the new soil requirements centered on the high level of expertise that would now be needed for soil analysis. Under the 1989 manual, soil criteria could be identified fairly easily by eye, but the Bush administration's plan called for carefully matching soil types to a long master list. Critics charged that this could be done only by people with extensive backgrounds in soil taxonomy. As a result, the delineation process would be much more cumbersome, time-consuming, and expensive.

Environmentalists stressed that these stringent prerequisites to any area's being declared a wetland would radically reduce protected acreage. They went on to point out the undesirable effects this would have.

For example, the 1991 proposals would probably result in much less protection for temporary and seasonal wetlands, which are often wet only during winter or early spring, outside the growing season. However, these are the very areas that ducks and other waterfowl depend on during migration. These birds— already documented at record lows due to previous habitat loss—would undoubtedly suffer further decreases in population.

Opening up formerly protected wetlands to development would mean more construction, including home building, in floodplains, exposing new home-owners to risk during high-water periods. In addition, also in terms of flood control, areas that might be excluded have a value equal to or greater than what the Bush administration was calling "real" wetlands—in fact, it's precisely because they are dry most of the year that they have a much larger capacity to absorb floodwater.

Environmentalists also publicized research that stated that removing the less wet wetlands from the protected roster would have a negative impact on bio-diversity, water quality, and fisheries.

Nevertheless, wetlands defenders tried to present their position as one that could exist peacefully with sensible development policies. They stressed that, under proper conditions, landowners could reap economic benefits from their holdings while still retaining the wetland function. Randy Lanctot, executive director of the Louisiana Wildlife Federation, observed that defining land "as wetlands doesn't mean banning it from development. It just means getting a permit in most cases. But the unfortunate part of reducing the scope of [wetlands] regulations is that this land will no longer have anyone with an interest in protecting the values of wetlands taking a look at it when the owner is changing the use of it."[6]

FALLOUT FROM THE AUGUST 1991 PROPOSALS

Conservation groups were not the only ones who discovered that the August 1991 proposals could mean an end to protection for vast tracts of the nation's wet-lands. When the EPA sent its own staff scientists out in the field to test the new guidelines, they reported back that the new rules could result in more than half of these areas being opened to development.

This finding gave fuel to those people within the Bush administration who were trying to modify the provisions. When the figures were released to the public (after the White House attempted to suppress them), they strengthened the large chorus of those who had spoken out against the government's plan. The review process was extended, and Congress entered the fray as well. It commissioned a study from the National Academy of Sciences, one that it hoped would settle some of the dispute over wetlands. This study, due in 1994, is intended to determine whether the current use of soil, vegetation, and hydrology criteria is a scientifically valid way to define a wetland.

Also in 1992 Congress required the Army Corps of Engineers to abandon the 1989 guidelines and return to its own 1987 delineation manual.

In fact, as the presidential campaign of 1992 moved into high gear, the administration's proposal was quietly put on hold. Nevertheless, it may have inflicted some political damage on the Bush-Quayle ticket. While conservatives were pleased with the government's easing up on environmental regulations in general, others took exception. Democratic nominee Governor Bill Clinton had had a mixed environmental record in Arkansas, but his running mate, Senator Al Gore, was particularly strong in this area. Reminding voters of George Bush's 1988 promise, their platform said that once they were in office they would make "the 'no net loss' wetlands pledge a reality" by basing "wetlands policy on science instead of politics."[7]

Just before the Democratic ticket took office in January 1993, EPA Administrator William Reilly ordered his agency to follow the 1987 Army Corps of Engineers manual as well. The August 1991 proposals, which had created so much controversy, were dead.

Both sides felt they had scored a victory. Those in favor of development or less government regulation were pleased that the 1989 guidelines had been abandoned. They vowed to continue to work to overturn laws they saw as too strict, and forged alliances with a number of members of Congress.

Environmentalists were happy to have stopped the 1991 redefinition. Some wetlands defenders took note of the fact that the Corps' 1987 manual didn't really differ that much from the 1989 guidelines. There were small differences in the technical steps taken in delineating a wetland, and some plants characterizing wetlands in the West were not included in the vegetation criteria. Their opponents may have perceived the 1987 manual as less strict, but perhaps that was because the Corps had often failed to enforce its regulations consistently before the 1989 guidelines took over.

In August 1993, the Clinton administration announced its own wetlands program. George Bush's campaign promise of "no net loss" was, for the first time, explicitly made national policy. A Bush administration proposal to exempt sections of the Alaskan tundra from protection was abandoned. While making it slightly harder for developers to build in certain wetlands, the Clinton plan also called for the establishment of new administrative channels for developers to appeal such decisions before going to court. The 1987 definition would continue to prevail until the National Academy of Sciences published its report. This policy drew some criticism from both sides, but administration officials hoped that it would become a new, fairly applied foundation for wetlands protection.

Meanwhile, Bill Clinton's appointment of Carol Browner as administrator of the EPA also suggested that a new era of realism and cooperation might be possible. A former aide to Vice President Gore, Browner has been characterized as "a new type of environmentalist who views economic development and environmental protection as compatible goals."[8] While head of Florida's Department of Environmental Regulation, Browner negotiated an agreement with the Walt Disney Company that allowed the corporation to fill in and develop 400 acres (162 hectares) of wetlands near Disney World in return for spending $40 million to buy a nearby 8,500-acre (3,400-hectare) ranch and restore it to its former wetland condition.

THE PROPERTY RIGHTS MOVEMENT

We have mentioned how various members of the business community—oil companies, shipping interests, and farmers—have tried to ensure that protection of these habitats did not take place at the expense of economic development. These parties often have enough influence to get their objections heard in the right places. On the other hand, smaller landowners generally have less opportunity to pressure a bureaucrat to step in and bend the rules. Consequently, they may be the target of stepped-up wetlands law enforcement more than the well-connected and influential are.

The case of a Morrisville, Pennsylvania, truck driver named John Pozsgai is instructive in this regard. A few years ago, Pozsgai bought a 14-acre (6-hectare) tract that had been used as a dumping ground for years. When he filled in the land, in preparation for building a garage, the Army Corps of Engineers told him to stop and apply for a permit. The work continued, and Pozsgai was eventually arrested, accused of forty-one counts of violating Section 404 of the Clean Water Act. Convicted, he was given a three-year jail term and fined more than $200,000.

Many environmentalists supported the verdict. Despite the land's obvious lack of esthetic attraction, it did have valuable flood-control functions. They also pointed out that Pozsgai had ignored the Army Corps of Engineers' "repeated warnings to cease and desist" filling in the wetland.[9] Others, however, had grave misgivings about one man's being punished so harshly, while corporations that violated environmental regulations often received mild fines. To them, Pozsgai became the most prominent martyr in the new property rights movement.

The property-rights movement (also called the wise-use movement) includes many small landowners who want their voices heard. (However, environmentalists claim that big business, such as mining and timber companies, have a significant behind-the-scenes role in these organizations.) More than 400 grass-roots groups have sprung up in recent years to help landowners facing problems with government regulations regarding land use. While regulations about historic preservation districts have been one target, wetlands laws are a primary focus of the small property owners who have joined this loose coalition. They contend that the government has been too restrictive in telling people what they can do with their own land. Often, a restriction on the use of a plot of land leads to a sharp decrease in property values.

The relationship of property values to property taxes is an area where this movement has enjoyed considerable success. In the United States, local governments—towns, school districts, and counties—derive much of their funding from taxes on land. These property taxes are levied on each parcel of land in a particular area, whether it is undeveloped, is farmed, or has offices, stores, or homes on it. Land owned by nonprofit organizations, such as churches or private universities, is usually exempted. Before levying these taxes, all tracts of land are assessed a value, and for undeveloped plots that assessment has traditionally been based on *the highest potential commercial value* of the site. The higher the assessment, the higher the tax.

Property-rights advocates say that wetlands protection statutes and other regulations on the future use of undeveloped land render the existing property-tax system unfair. They argue that if one branch of the government restricts the development of your land, other sectors of the government should not tax it as if you could soon take advantage of its maximum commercial potential.

This argument has now reached the nation's courts. In April 1992, a judge in New Jersey reviewed the property-tax bill on an undeveloped 240-acre (97-hectare) parcel of land in the Hackensack River Meadowlands; the tract was assessed at $20 million and property taxes were $300,000 each year. Acknowledging that federal and state restrictions rendered the land basically undevelopable, the judge rolled the assessed value of the land back to $976,000, and the annual local property taxes were thereby reduced to $17,000. Elsewhere, local governments have acknowledged that environmentally crucial land has no development potential—assessments and taxes have been slashed in such places as Anchorage, Alaska; Bryan County, Georgia; and Staten Island, New York.

Meanwhile, other property-rights advocates have focused on the regulations themselves. After a developer named David Lucas bought two expensive oceanfront lots outside Charleston, South Carolina, his plan to build expensive houses was stalled. The state's Beachfront Management Law, administered by the South Carolina Coastal Council, restricted coastal development. Lucas sued the council, saying that the regulation amounted to a "taking," referring to the Fifth Amendment of the U.S. Constitution, which prohibits the government from taking private property without compensating the landowner. He argued that, even though he retained his land, the restrictions the state applied amounted to an unconstitutional taking. South Carolina courts ruled that Lucas was not entitled to compensation, so he appealed to the United States Supreme Court. When the Lucas case reached the Supreme Court in June 1992, the Court did not deliver the broad, definitive ruling that both sides had hoped for; instead the case was returned to a lower court for additional review. Nonetheless, this is but one of many lawsuits now before American courts that present a formidable challenge from property-rights advocates to wetlands laws (as well as to laws affecting landmarks and historic preservation districts).

Even as wetlands protections currently seem safe under the Clinton administration, property-rights advocates will continue to battle these and other regulations before local zoning boards, in courts, and before the state and federal governments. They have two important things on their side. First, public opinion tends to favor the little guy, so a small landowner battling government regulations inspires more sympathy than a large corporation attempting to overturn those same regulations. If laws are changed as a result, however, big business may also benefit. Second, the right to own private property, with a minimum of restrictions on its use, is virtually enshrined in America, as it is in most Western democracies.

THE EVERGLADES AND OTHER WETLANDS

While laws and other regulations to protect swamps, marshes, and bogs have had a major impact on some habitats, for others the increased consciousness about the value of these areas may be a case of too little, too late. In order to help preserve the nation's most vital wetlands over the coming generations, it's important to look at some typical American wetlands close-up, to see how each ecosystem's survival has been linked to developments on the broader stage of human events.

THE EVERGLADES

TOPOGRAPHY AND HISTORY
The Everglades originally comprised more than 2 million acres (810,000 hectares), covering all of central and southern Florida except for a ridge of upland along the Atlantic coast. The most famous of American wetlands, it combines marsh and swamp areas and is part of the drainage system for Lake Okeechobee, which sits only 19 feet (5.8 m) above sea level. That lake, the largest lake in the southern half of the United States, receives much of its water

103

from smaller lakes to the north, almost as far as Orlando.

Before humans began to interfere with water supplies in south Florida (to meet the needs of a population explosion that started in the middle of the twentieth century), that drainage system worked as follows: Whenever Lake Okeechobee got too full—especially during the rainier summer months—it would overflow, and water began a slow trip to the sea. Because most of south Florida is near sea level, this sheet of water didn't channel neatly into rivers flowing downhill toward the Gulf of Mexico. Instead, it would spread out along the large plain of the Everglades (to as much as 50 miles [80.5 km] wide, although it was rarely deeper than 6 inches [15 cm]). Then the water would move very slowly through vast expanses of marsh grasses. In effect, much of the Everglades was, in the words of naturalist and writer Marjory Stoneman Douglas, a "river of grass."

To this day, other terrain interrupts the enormous, sawgrass-dominated freshwater floodplain. Willow and bay trees rise out of the marsh, and little islands known as heads develop around them, built up from sediment trapped from the water flowing by. On slightly higher ground—perhaps 1 to 3 feet (0.3 to 1 m) above the glades—groves of subtropical trees give a more swamplike feel; these rises are called hammocks. Cypress swamps cover huge portions of the Everglades, especially on the western edge (which includes the half-million-acre [200,500-hectare] Big Cypress National Preserve). As the sheet of water nears the shoreline, saline mangrove swamps take over as the prevailing habitat. This unique marsh-swamp combination is home to vast numbers of plant forms and wildlife, including a variety of subtropical and tropical species found nowhere else in the continental United States. Most of the wildlife has made special

Sawgrass covers much of the Everglades, the largest wetland in North America.

adaptations to the highs and lows of the water supply pulsing through the Everglades. (For more on plants and wildlife in the area, see the species descriptions in chapter 3.)

THE TIDE OF DEVELOPMENT

Early development in south Florida concentrated on the coastal ridge along the Atlantic Ocean. The Everglades themselves were hardly a hospitable home for settlers, although some wetlands were drained and converted to agricultural use. Two floods after hurricanes, one in 1925 and the second in 1928, killed about 2,500 people in the sparsely populated region.

In the next decade, the population of south Florida began to mushroom, as people from the Midwest and Northeast, attracted by the warm climate, moved south. By the time another destructive storm, in 1947, flooded wide swathes of farmland, pressures had mounted for a comprehensive water-management system. The Army Corps of Engineers embarked on an ambitious plan: by building a network of canals, levees, and pumping stations, the Corps said, floods could be prevented, farmland could be irrigated, and the growing population could be guaranteed an adequate water supply, even during the dryer winter months. At the same time, Congress created the Everglades National Park, occupying less than one-fifth of the original Everglades. The Corps' plan included supplying water to the park as well, while preventing salt water's intrusion on the system from the ocean (a problem because the land is so flat and the groundwater level is so close to the sea).

As part of this project, the Corps converted the Kissimmee River, which had meandered along its 92-mile (148-km) course south from Lake Kissimmee to Lake Okeechobee, into a 50-mile-long (80 km) ditch the Corps called Canal 38. This work opened up vast areas south of Orlando to development—a large tract just south of Lake Okeechobee, christened the Everglades Agricultural Area, was drained. It's now part of a vast agricultural tract that specializes in sugarcane and provides the majority of the winter produce sold in North America. Between the agricultural area to the north and the park in the southwest corner of the Everglades lay a series of water-management districts, all managed by a state body called the South Florida Water Management District.

This elaborate system, which includes 1,400 miles (2,250 km) of canals, was built between 1947 and the late 1960s. However, the basic problem with it has been that it has starved the Everglades themselves of water. South Florida has continued to boom: the region is now home to almost 5 million people, and about 1,000 newcomers arrive each day. The pressures of commercial, agricultural, and residential development also continue, as more wetlands are drained and converted to other uses and the need for fresh water increases.

Meanwhile, it turned out to be very expensive to release water into the park, so the water district's managers let fresh water flow out to the sea instead. A series of dry years in the 1960s exacerbated the situation, so that this fragile ecosystem was on the brink of collapse.

In the 1970s, an infant environmental movement in south Florida turned back a proposal to build a new Miami airport in the Everglades. Since then, it has helped pass laws mandating that at least a minimum amount of water flow into the natural areas of the glades. Nonetheless, the unabated tide of development in the region created additional pressures.

As a result, bird censuses showed dramatically low counts, down 80 to 95 percent from levels recorded in the 1930s. There were more endangered or threatened

Pollution from agricultural areas to the north and the demand for water to serve residential areas to the east threaten the unspoiled stretches of Everglades National Park.

species in Florida than in any other state in the nation. Agricultural runoff—the excess from irrigated farmlands, which flowed back into the aquifer—brought with it huge amounts of phosphorus and nitrogen that the natural cleansing abilities of the wetlands couldn't absorb. A little to the north, in Lake Okeechobee, these minerals settled at the lake bottom, hastening eutrophication. Eutrophication is the process by which a lake becomes nutrient rich but oxygen poor; the lack of oxygen kills fish and much plant life. In the Everglades themselves, the nutrient-rich runoff also affected the mixture of plant life, as phosphorus-loving cattails overwhelmed competing plants.

STEPS TOWARD A COMEBACK
By the 1980s, there was enough concern about the future of the Everglades that a broad-based coalition—embracing various community members, from fervent environmentalists to politicians—was able to coalesce around a proposal to save the Everglades. Former Florida governor Bob Graham led the effort to persuade the Army Corps of Engineers to undo some of its work. Most notably, the Corps was asked to de-channelize Canal 38 in an attempt to re-create the original winding path of the Kissimmee River. By late 1992, a test project was pronounced a success, so the Corps and the state of Florida hope to proceed with this ambitious effort.

Another part of the plan was the construction of a new levee on the eastern edge of the park. It is hoped that this levee will keep enough water inside wild areas. The government also purchased more than 105,000 acres (42,500 hectares) to expand the park (some to preserve in a natural state, and others to reclaim as wetlands).

While measures like these were being implemented in an attempt to halt the ecosystem's imminent death, the coalition was aiming higher, hoping to restore the Everglades to its former glory. But it was no simple task to reverse years of damage, and impediments appeared from all sides, including some from unexpected quarters.

People who had moved into the eastern fringe of the Everglades from the Atlantic coast opposed plans to expand the park or to revert to a more natural water flow. They demanded full compensation for any land that the state repossessed or for any flood damage resulting from increasing water flow into the glades.

Sugarcane producers felt the state of Florida was trying to saddle them with much of the costs of saving the Everglades. In 1991, the state admitted that it had failed to protect the glades from phosphorus runoff from sugarcane fields. In agreeing to a legal settlement that slashed the amount of phosphorus that could enter the ecosystem, the South Florida Water Management District promised to convert land it bought back from farmers to filtration marshes, where phosphorus-loving plants, like cattails, would remove most of the mineral before it entered wilder areas. A new state law allowed the water district to pay for all this by assessing the sugarcane producers for each ton of phosphorus they discharged into public canals.[1] The sugarcane producers, who had earlier objected to the dechannelization of Canal 38, protested loudly. They claimed that it was the state's mismanagement of water supplies that had caused the damage.

At the same time, park officials and ecologists realized that their early attempts to re-create the natural flow of water through the river of grass presented unforeseen problems. In the 1980s, a new water-delivery program, designed to mimic natural patterns, increased the sheet flow. But it also allowed for additional releases if flooding concerns warranted. Biologists soon saw that this caused water levels to rise in

110

areas where wading birds fed and nested, further depressing their small numbers. As one park official said, "Everybody thought it was all just a problem of water volume. They didn't realize that the distribution and timing of water flow were just as important. The nesting colonies began to fade away."[2]

As they modified the plan, the needs of the wood stork, an endangered wading bird, became another concern. Its nesting impulse seems to be triggered by the concentration of fish populations in sloughs during the dry season. To simulate the natural patterns this bird needed for successful breeding, park and water district officials diverted flow from an area just north of the park called Water Conservation Area 3A. However, 3A was crucial to the survival of the snail kite, another endangered bird; its principal food, the apple snail, needs wet conditions in 3A, its major habitat. Thus what's beneficial to the wood stork and other waders—diverting water from 3A—works to the detriment of another endangered species, the snail kite. Some ecologists point out that in the past, because of weather conditions and without human interference, the populations of one bird would boom while the other fell, and vice versa. Chances are that there will be other stumbling blocks as the Everglades water plan is gradually put into effect.

Hurricane Andrew, which struck south Florida in August 1992, proved an unexpected, mixed blessing. Soon after the storm, park officials estimated that it would cost $27 million to replace or fix facilities damaged or ruined by the hurricane. At the same time, this provided an opportunity to rethink what the parks in the Everglades can and should be. Repairable structures were fixed to reopen the park. However, for buildings that were destroyed, officials promised to determine whether a replacement was even needed. If a new structure was deemed necessary, they said they would carefully evaluate the building; if possible, new construction would be smaller and would intrude less on the environment.

Another long-term concern was the millions of trees that had been knocked down by the severe storm. Of course, hurricanes are part of the natural cycle of this large wetland, as are fires caused by lightning, and the way they clear out heavily forested areas gives other species a chance to flourish. However, the danger is that exotic species brought to south Florida by homeowners and gardeners—like the melaleuca, the Australian pine, the Florida holly, the paperbark, and the Brazilian peppertree—would proliferate. In the wake of Hurricane Andrew, winds may carry these seeds from the coastal ridge west into the Everglades, where they could, as a parks spokesman said, "grow like wildfire and drive out the native vegetation."[3] Reports of the storm's effect on wildlife were slow in coming, so it may take years to fully assess its impact on the area's ecological balance.

LOUISIANA'S COASTAL WETLANDS

While the changes in south Florida provide hope that the Everglades can be saved, the situation looks worse in Louisiana. Forty percent of America's coastal wetlands are found in this state, but they are still being lost at a rate of 50 square miles (130 sq km) a year—and not, as is so often the case elsewhere, because of development that promises to create needed jobs. Here, the majority of the acreage is being reclaimed by the sea. In the lowermost portion of the Mississippi River Delta, the U.S. Fish and Wildlife Service estimated that from 1956 to 1983, 48 percent of the land was lost to the sea.

These areas had been a spectacularly rich habitat—breeding ground for almost all of the fish and shellfish

112

Low-lying areas in the Mississippi River delta are often buffeted by flooding after hurricanes and offshore storms.

harvested commercially in the Gulf of Mexico, winter resting place for huge numbers of waterfowl, and home to many reptiles and mammals, including those of value to the fur industry such as nutria and mink. In addition, they protected New Orleans and smaller communities from the full fury of coastal hurricanes.

The principal cause of the shrinkage of Louisiana's wetlands has been the damming, channelization, and leveeing of the Mississippi River. Dams upstream reduce the amount of sediment the river brings downstream. Levees prevent the rich sediment that still makes it downriver from being deposited in the marsh to help build the area up; instead, it's flushed out into the Gulf of Mexico. The leveeing of the Mississippi also prevents sediment from reaching bottomland swamps just north of the coastal wetlands. They too are now threatened.

The main channel of the Mississippi remains navigable to oceangoing vessels, and Louisiana's large oil and natural gas industries have sliced other large canals through the marshes. Not only do these waterways make it easy for tidal surges following coastal hurricanes to threaten residential areas, they also allow salt water to invade the marshes, killing freshwater vegetation and increasing erosion.

In a state that for the most part has been, as one writer put it, "prodigal with its natural resources"[4] and where petrochemical and shipping industries have exerted tremendous power, a conservation ethic has been slow to arise. Recently, a local coalition has begun working with the state government on a series of short-term steps to improve the health of the coastal marshes. At the same time, it is trying to rally support for big, long-term projects like those currently under way in the Everglades, which may reverse some of the alterations of the past. Only time will tell if Louisiana's coastal wetlands will survive, or whether this is all a case of too little, too late.

ARCATA MARSH AND OTHER SUCCESS STORIES

While the Everglades suffered the ill effects of too much phosphorus in its runoff, a small town across the country in northern California was demonstrating how a wetland habitat can absorb pollutants. Arcata, a town of 15,000 located on Humboldt Bay, 280 miles (448 km) north of San Francisco, is home to a complex of salt- and freshwater marshes that host thousands of birds, hundreds of naturalists and picnickers, and a municipal salmon hatchery. But these marshes are all part of the municipal sewage treatment facility. Wastewater from the town's sewage processing plant flows through this coastal wetland and after two months what is discharged into the bay more than exceeds water pollution standards.

It all started in the mid-1970s. The sewage treatment plant in Arcata, like many municipal facilities in North America, incorporated two oxidation ponds. After solids were removed in the plant itself, the wastewater was pumped into these open, artificial ponds, where many algae and other microbes were rendered harmless. Nevertheless, California's state water control board ruled that the effluent the town then discharged into the bay was no longer clean enough. The board presented plans to construct a larger modern treatment facility for Arcata and two neighboring towns. Local citizens balked at the high price tag and potential environmental costs.

Based on an undergraduate's suggestion, two professors at the local university devised an imaginative alternative solution. Arcata would create a wetland, and after wastewater went through the plant (which would be upgraded) and the oxidation ponds, it would be filtered through that wetland. The algae and other potentially dangerous microbes would be eaten by other small organisms in the soil or absorbed as

115

nutrients by wetland plants. After this natural cleansing the water would then be discharged into the bay.

The state water control board was not receptive to
this innovative plan, failing to see how the water discharged into Humboldt Bay could be clean enough.
But Arcata persisted and a small pilot project was ap-
proved in 1979. On a run-down 32-acre (13-hectare)
site next to the oxidation ponds that had once been
home to a dump, a lumber mill, and a railroad trestle,
a complex that included a new lake and freshwater
marshes was carefully constructed. As the demonstration began to treat wastewater, an adjacent salt marsh
was restored. The town also purchased nearby uplands to create a stretch of open space around the
wetlands, building duck blinds and picnic areas in the
process.

By 1983 the state reviewed results from the pilot
project and gave the go-ahead for Arcata's full-scale
plan. Three years later, treated effluent entered the
wetland for the first time. The results have confirmed
the wisdom of the project. When water enters the bay
from the wetland, it is cleaner than state standards for
discharge from sewage treatment facilities. Not only
has the project cost much less than the regional facility
the state water control board proposed, but Arcata has
gained more than 100 acres (40 hectares) of open park-
land. Town officials say they couldn't have afforded to
provide these recreational opportunities otherwise.

More than 200 species of birds have been sighted
in the marsh, which has now become an important
stop along the Pacific flyway; as a result, Arcata is now
a mecca for West Coast bird-watchers. There's also a
salmon hatchery growing fish in the wastewater. Out
in the bay itself, the oyster beds continue to thrive,
proving once more that the wastewater is clean and
also preserving jobs for the local fishing industry.

In addition, Arcata Marsh attracts a steady stream

More than 4 miles (6.4 km) of nature trails cross the marsh that the town of Arcata, California, has built to treat its wastewater.

of a different kind of tourist: government officials and ecologists interested in the sewage treatment project. Local officials claim that similar setups would work in larger towns, too. What's needed is both oxidation ponds and an adequate amount of low-lying public wetlands; being next to the seacoast is not a necessity. They caution, however, that such systems can't process untreated industrial wastewater and storm drainage, both of which can alter the delicate mix of microbes and water needed for a wetland to filter out pollutants successfully.

In fact, similar projects are now being considered throughout North America. In High River, Alberta, wastewater from a meat-processing plant and the town itself is piped after treatment to a created wetland.

Officials in Sierra Vista, Arizona, hope to create a sewage marsh similar to Arcata's along the banks of the San Pedro River. However, they are currently stymied by stringent EPA wastewater regulations concerning discharge into a body of water that may contain endangered species (as does the San Pedro); in such cases water must meet stricter standards than what is considered safe to drink.

Outside Orlando, Florida, lies a 1,200-acre (486-hectare) wetland created in the late 1980s. Treated effluent is pumped 14 miles (22.5 km) from the city to the marsh, which was constructed on a cow pasture (which had itself been a wetland before it was drained for ranching in the nineteenth century). The 13 million gallons (49.2 million l) introduced into the marsh daily make their way through three distinct habitats—a marsh dominated by cattails and bulrushes, a second marsh featuring a mixture of plant life, and a hardwood swamp—as nitrates, phosphates, and other wastes are absorbed naturally. As in Arcata, the marsh teems with birds, wildlife, and plant life, and the exiting water meets or exceeds the mandated standards. While the water discharged in Orlando goes into the Saint Johns River, which flows north, the project is being closely studied by scientists and officials working just to the south to save the Everglades.

THE CORPS SWITCHES GEAR

A project under way on the Mississippi River just north of St. Louis is representative of the changes at the Army Corps of Engineers. By replacing locks and a dam near Alton, Illinois, the Corps is also initiating an environmental management program to lessen the heavy toll its huge public works projects have traditionally exacted on nature.

At Alton, the Corps acquired 2 square miles (5.2 sq km) of farmland to restore as the wetlands they once had been. The majority of these bottomlands will be a low, wet prairie, with 300 acres (122 hectares) set aside for a marsh. A small lake will complement the basin created by the dam itself, drawing migrating waterfowl to the area. Biologists are being consulted about the topography of these habitats, about which seeds to plant where, and so on; scientists will monitor the restoration, especially during the crucial initial period.

The entire project, called the Riverlands Environmental Demonstration Area, represents an opportunity for the Corps to prove that it's serious about balancing ecological and engineering concerns. It is hoped that many of the more than 2 million residents of the St. Louis metropolitan area will visit Riverlands to appreciate the wildlife the wetland will attract. A nature trail will make portions of the site accessible to tourists. Of the Corps' own "green" evolution, Colonel James Corbin, the head of the St. Louis district office during the planning stages of the Riverlands project, said, "It won't happen overnight, but it's certainly moving in that direction."[5]

It would seem that even while the debate over protection for wetlands in private hands continues to rage, a broad consensus has emerged that wetlands owned by federal, state, or local governments should be preserved as much as possible. Nevertheless, difficult decisions remain. Often the choice is between preservation and job prospects for area residents, but at other times ecological considerations raise additional problems.

As with the wood stork and the snail kite in the Everglades, the environmental movement has to face painful dilemmas about competing needs. In Nevada, for instance, two national wildlife refuges near Stillwater (one an important stop for migrating birds on the Pacific flyway) have seen their water supplies threatened. The wetlands in both refuges are fed by water from a regional irrigation district. Meanwhile, the cui-ui, a small fish on the endangered species lists, spawns in the lower reaches of the Truckee River. To ensure good conditions for successful breeding, water must be diverted from the irrigation district to the river. The resulting loss to the Stillwater wetlands, aggravated by a drought that began in the late 1980s, may be as high as 95 percent.

6

MITIGATION

While political debates continue over the government's definition of wetlands, and the efforts to save large tracts such as the Everglades garner attention in nationwide media, the fate of North America's wetlands is also dependent on what happens to thousands of small plots of land scattered across the continent, many of them in private hands.

Those property owners who want to maximize the economic value of their land, by opening it up to commercial, industrial, or residential development, continue to file for permits with the Army Corps of Engineers and then with local and county planning and building departments. Often, the Corps or a local authority works with the permit seeker to minimize the impact a proposed development may have on a wetland.

Let's suppose a developer applies for a permit to build a complex of homes and stores on a large site, only a quarter of which is wetland. The principal road into the site will slice through the wetland. If plans call for half of that wetland to be filled in to provide for this road, the Corps might suggest that it be rerouted to another part of the site. In that way, the entire wetland could be preserved—something the developer might very well agree to do in order to secure permission to build on the larger tract of the land.

If, for whatever reason, it's not possible to move the road entirely out of the wetland, the Corps may persuade the developer to move it to the border, right next to the uplands, so that a larger portion of the wetland is preserved and the surviving habitat is not bisected by a road. Once the authorities and the developer agree, the necessary changes are made, the permit is granted, and construction begins. As mentioned earlier, the Corps grants permits to the majority of those who seek them. But, because the Corps has this kind of input into the project, it should be clear that it does not rubber-stamp projects that seek large alterations of wetlands.

In fact, some wise developers are using the government's modification of their plans to their advantage, promoting the new homes they've built as respectful of the surrounding environment. In affluent Pound Ridge, New York, a development company turned the table on town planners. It persuaded the town to drop the main road in its master plan for the 263-acre (107-hectare) site in favor of five cul-de-sacs. This enabled the developer to preserve 32 acres (13 hectares) of wetlands and maintain other natural areas on the site. Once the subdivision was built, its ecologically sensitive planning became a key selling point to potential home buyers.

In cases like these, where the permit seeker and the authorities are able to agree on a feasible approach, wetlands are saved as economic development continues. However, there are times when it's simply not possible to avoid harming a wetland in the course of development. Sometimes the government itself is the culprit, as when a road must be widened for highway safety or to ease traffic congestion. Mitigation is the answer in these cases. Mitigation is a way to compensate for the destruction of a wetland (or a portion of one) by enhancing, restoring, or creating a similar-sized habitat nearby. (Some people consider the type of design modifications in the Pound Ridge development a type of mitigation.)

Enhancing is an attempt to improve on the qualities of an existing wetland. The habitat may have mediocre plant or wildlife populations, or it may be disturbed during the process of construction in adjacent uplands. New plants, preferably ones that are native to wetlands in the general area, are carefully introduced. Judicious alterations, such as nesting platforms for waterfowl, may be made to attract more wildlife. The focus of enhancement is on upgrading a wetland that may not currently have an exceptional natural value. This approach is not favored in some states.

We have seen examples of restoration in the last chapter: the lands added to the Everglades, the coastal marsh in Arcata, and the riverside marsh near Alton. You may also recall the deal that EPA Administrator Carol Browner made with the Walt Disney Company when she headed Florida's Department of Environmental Regulation: 8,500 acres (3,400 hectares) of ranch land near Disney World will be purchased by that company, turned back into wetlands, and maintained, in exchange for permission to fill in a 400-acre (162-hectare) wetland.

In all these cases, habitats that were converted for human use anywhere from a few decades to two centuries ago are now reclaimed and turned back into wetlands. While the predisposition of the soil toward wet conditions may provide a head start, these sites must be closely watched to ensure that they thrive. For example, some states require three years of monitoring and filing of follow-up reports.

Riparian wetlands flanking western rivers are dry most of the year.

Creating a wetland—making a bona fide marsh or swamp on a site that has always been upland—is an even more difficult and expensive task, one that requires extraordinarily careful planning, meticulous execution, and extensive monitoring. Generally, the developer must create an equal amount of new wetland for each acre on the site that is going to be dredged, drained, or filled. Some states mandate a 2:1 ratio—2 new acres for each destroyed acre.

"AN ART AS WELL AS A SCIENCE"

Mitigation of any kind is an expensive process. Design work and construction alone can run from $50,000 to $125,000 an acre; engineering fees, land costs, and the purchase of wetlands plants are extra.

In examining mitigation in detail, it's important to keep in mind that the process is largely regulated by the states; therefore, procedures and rules vary widely. For instance, New Jersey encourages mitigation sites adjacent to, or at least in the same watershed as, the tract being developed. Next door in Pennsylvania, however, the state allows a restored wetland in the Poconos as mitigation for a filled-in swamp 100 miles (161 km) to the south in Philadelphia.

While specific projects vary even more than state laws do, the steps in a mitigation project generally include the following: As the development gets under way, the group in charge brings in a team of trained specialists—engineers, ecologists, landscapers, and others—to look closely at the site where mitigation is taking place. After an extensive survey, the new wetland is designed, incorporating the topography of the land, the plant life, and the hydrology pattern. Designing a workable system of hydrology is perhaps the most crucial task: seasonal and annual variations in water level, the depth and volume of water on the site, and other considerations must be taken into account.

125

Construction comes next, which can range from little more than filling in drainage ditches on converted farmland to trucking in suitable soils and remaking the landscape when creating a brand-new wetland. The wetland vegetation is then planted, often after having been transported hundreds of miles from specialized nurseries that grow the plants in carefully matched wetland soils. Afterward, weeding to prevent invasion of undesirable species is still necessary. The amount of monitoring and follow-up reports depends on the location of the project and the nature of the work itself. Only after the vegetation has established itself does wildlife return.

PROBLEMS WITH MITIGATION

Wetland mitigation is a new, inexact science, and one engineer observes that it's "an art as well as a science."[1] Nevertheless, enough projects have been executed that those involved in the field have identified several recurring problems.

A study of mitigation commissioned by the EPA found that a long-term commitment to monitor and manage the project was key to success. As a rule, government bodies or private conservation groups turn out to be better supervisors than private developers. All too often, a developer who received permission to build on a huge tract of property in exchange for mitigation nearby doesn't allow for follow-up and may even walk away from the wetland once construction is complete. In addition, the problem may be compounded by an initial decision to save money by hiring an inexperienced team—for instance, only landscapers who have no background in wetlands ecology, and no ecologists or specially trained engineers. The work of such a team can do more harm than good.

Some states have mandated a longer period of follow-through so mitigation projects will be supervised better. In New Jersey, for instance, three years of monitoring, including regularly filed reports, must come after any restoration project. Nonetheless, experts say that the best mitigation work is done by developers who strive to exceed the requirements of the law.

The inexperience of some people working in the field has also been a problem. In such a tricky discipline, a lack of training can be very harmful. Frequently the result is a flawed design that never has clearly defined goals. Joy Zedler, a wetlands ecologist who has been critical of much mitigation work, says, "It isn't enough that it looks green. It has to be a functional ecosystem. Two mediocre man-made acres don't make up for one natural."[2]

Zedler's reservations may stem in part from follow-up monitoring she is doing on a restored marsh at Chula Vista, California, near San Diego; after five years this mitigation project, ordered by a federal court when the state wanted to build a new highway interchange, remains far from its goals. She wonders whether success will prove more elusive on projects stemming from a government-regulated settlement, "where restoration becomes a license to destroy habitat somewhere else."[3]

There are also inherent limitations to what mitigation can accomplish. Coastal wetlands are easier to restore, since the ebb and flow of tides make for a predictable pattern of water levels. In creating freshwater wetlands, one must depend on rain and groundwater, both of which fluctuate seasonally and annually. Swamps are much harder to restore than marshes, simply because the trees common there take years to mature. Therefore, it's just not possible to gauge if the project has taken hold well for more than a generation.

As mentioned earlier, creating a new wetland is far

more difficult than restoring one, where a parcel of land that had once been wetland is returned to its original condition. In the latter case, the soils are already predisposed to wetness and the types of vegetation that favor saturated soil will thrive once they are reintroduced. By contrast, an upland plot designated for mitigation doesn't have inherent wetlands characteristics. To create a marsh there will probably require extensive regrading, the importation of special wetlands soils, and other modifications. With no natural affinity toward being a wetland, it is harder to make it one.

Another impediment is that there is no one definition of successful mitigation. In fact, critics point out that it will take hundreds, or even thousands, of years to see if a specific artificially altered ecosystem will function as well as a similar one never affected by human activity. Even in the short term, no overall standards for success yet exist. In the meantime, some mitigation specialists say there is now enough of a track record to create a yardstick against which new projects can be judged (after one year, certain criteria should be reached, and so on).

Those involved in mitigation observe that the process itself is here to stay. They realize that development and growth will continue to be part of the North American economy, and that not every wetland can be protected from the bulldozers of progress. The process still needs to be improved and refined. However, when done properly, mitigation is one way to preserve wetlands and all their advantages to society, from waterfowl habitat and biodiversity to flood control and recreational uses.

Mitigation advocates point with pride to the record of Ed Garbisch, a former chemistry professor whose Maryland firm has restored or created more than 350 projects since the early 1970s; he has a success rate of

97 percent. When mitigation is well managed—with careful attention paid every step of the way from the initial design through to monitoring and follow-up after construction—it serves a necessary function in preserving wetlands while not standing in the way of economic growth and jobs.

THE PULL OF THE FREE MARKET

MITIGATION BANKING

In recent years, representatives from some environmental groups, government, and industry have worked together to find a method of harnessing free-market forces for the good of the environment. One of the plans they've come up with is called mitigation banking, which works as follows:

Imagine that a private conservation organization acquires a parcel of land that had once been wetlands and then restores it. The group is then allocated a certain amount of credits at a central registry called a mitigation bank. Meanwhile, a developer wants to fill in a marsh and build homes there; she must find a parcel of land nearby on which to restore or create a mitigating wetland before she can receive her permit to alter the marsh. Unable to locate a suitable plot herself, she buys credits at the mitigation bank—in other words, she makes a payment to cover the cost of the credits the private conservation organization has earned. She then obtains her permit and construction begins. In effect, the developer has paid, after the fact, for the private group's restoration work on another site.

Supporters of the mitigation banking concept say that it is a practical solution to a thorny problem. Among other things, the restored wetlands remain the responsibility of the conservation group, which is more likely to have a long-term commitment to monitoring conditions in the ecosystem carefully and managing it well. However, some critics in the environmental community suggest that mitigation banking is merely a cynical method of destroying pristine wetlands by letting developers buy a substitute habitat, one that is often inferior. The developer has little incentive to avoid altering untouched habitats, the way she might when working with the Army Corps of Engineers and state or local planning boards during the permit process.

POLLUTION CREDITS

The use of pollution credits is another new way in which economists are trying to reduce environmental damage. Although we have yet to see a wide use of pollution credits to help save wetlands, market-based solutions like it have already been implemented to reduce air pollution. The 1990 Clean Air Act authorized the EPA to initiate an emissions credit program for utilities. Since early 1992, utilities have been contracting with one another to buy and sell these credits. This is how it works:

Each utility is assigned a limit to the amount of sulfur dioxide it may emit into the atmosphere. If a utility's amount of discharge is reduced below that ceiling, it receives credits. If a utility's discharges exceed the ceiling, it pays a hefty fine or it can buy discharge credits from the other companies that have them. It will then have to pay for enough credits to offset the excess pounds of sulfur dioxide in its emissions.

The utility with the extremely clean operation is rewarded financially for reducing its pollution below the limit. The second company pays the price, and has an economic incentive to improve its performance in the future. The EPA is freed of much regulatory responsibility, as the utilities decide themselves how they will meet their limit, either by reducing emissions or by buying credits from others who have done so.

Similarly, southern California authorities are letting factories trade so-called smog futures in the marketplace as the region tries to improve its air quality.

Pollution credits and mitigation banking are just two of the innovative methods environmental economists are promoting. As mentioned in chapter 2, it has traditionally been difficult to assign a specific monetary value to wildlife refuges and other natural habitats. This has complicated the battle to save wetlands, since the developers usually are able to cite how much money a specific project will bring in to a community and how many jobs will be created, both in the construction itself and once the project is finished. Especially in a period of slow economic growth and widespread unemployment, it is hard for environmentalists to counter these compelling arguments and make the case for preserving wetlands. Solutions such as mitigation banking that employ free-enterprise models to make the world greener may be the wave of the future.

7

THE FUTURE OF WETLANDS

The disappearance of wetlands is a problem that exists worldwide, not only in the United States and Canada. These habitats are found on every continent except Antarctica. In countries all over the world, there are similar pressures to open up wetlands to development. Around the globe, the same issues—the competing needs of protecting the environment and encouraging economic growth, of preserving biodiversity while irrigating nearby fields, of providing natural flood control and finding new jobs—come into play.

The developed nations have already sheltered some wetlands from development. The two largest wetlands in Europe—La Camargue, just west of Marseilles, France, and the Coto de Doñana, a marsh at the delta of Spain's Guadalquivir River—are both national parks.

The latter, which covers 125,000 acres (50,625 hectares), is home or resting place to about 1 million birds each year. But at Doñana the pressures of human development are threatening the large buffer zone that surrounds the park. There are plans to build a series of resort hotels, with accompanying marinas, golf courses, and other facilities. Nearby farms growing vegetables are asking for more water, although studies have shown that irrigation has already affected the water table, so that some lagoons have dried up. And agricultural runoff entering the marsh has shown high levels of pollutants.[1]

In the industrialized countries of Western Europe, as in North America, there is some consensus about the value of preserving nature. However, in the so-called developing countries, the arguments of environmentalists about the virtues of conservation carry less weight. In general, these countries have different priorities. Economic growth, which has traditionally brought with it industrialization, large-scale production technologies, and gigantic dams and other public works projects, is favored. With a significant proportion of the population living in or close to poverty (and often threatened with starvation or disease), the need to foster a modern economy and create jobs takes precedence over environmental considerations.

Advisers from international aid agencies and the developed countries of the West offer well-meaning advice on how natural resources should be managed, hoping the Third World will avoid some of the trespasses the West committed against the environment. However, history makes it hard for the governments of less-developed countries to listen. All too often, the industrialized world's suggestions carry a "do as we say, not as we did" tone. Developing countries often regard that attitude as both paternalistic—carrying an uncomfortable echo of colonial times—and unrealistic. Why, they counter, should we not reap the same economic benefits from our natural resources that you did from your own?

As a result, it is sometimes difficult for conservationists to get their cases heard in the Third World. In the Mexican state of Sonora, for example, the Soldado estuary is the target for a development including a marina, hotels, and homes, all intended to spur tourism and economic growth. The project will create 18,000 construction jobs, as well as many others once the facilities are complete. Opponents of the project admit that in a poor area like this, saving the breeding grounds and habitat of fish and birds may have to take a backseat to economic development.

The use of environmental economics may be a more effective way to stop such projects, or at least to encourage design changes that will reduce harm to wetland habitats. Environmentalists are marshaling such arguments at a project in northern Nigeria. A series of dams and irrigation projects threatens the Hadejia-Nguru wetlands, a floodplain that serves as a buffer zone between a river system flowing into Lake Chad and the desert. Currently, each year's floods recharge the groundwater and water table, ensuring adequate supplies from wells year-round. As more dams are completed upstream, however, these supplies are dwindling. Some observers fear that these wetlands, once the site of many productive small farms and already shrinking, will wind up as desert.

For the past twenty years, the Nigerian government and its Western advisers have tried to regulate water flow by building dams and digging canals for massive irrigation projects. By now, the water table in some areas has fallen by more than 25 yards (22.9 m). Severe droughts in recent years have made the direct effect of the completed damming hard to calculate. However, a study done for a private Nigerian conservation group suggests that the water projects are responsible for half of the damage.[2]

Those working to stop further damming observe that completed projects rarely deliver the lavish increases in agricultural productivity that are promised before ground is broken. Such dams and irrigation works may actually be a poor use of capital investment for a developing nation such as Nigeria. Opponents of the effort have estimated that for every acre of fields irrigated by one project upstream, more than two acres of Hadejia-Nguru wetlands were lost. Another study showed that although these public works accounted for the vast majority of government investment in agriculture in the 1980s, the farmlands whose thirst they nourished produced about 5 percent of Nigeria's total crop output. By contrast, nature irrigates the small fields in what floodplains and wetlands survive at no charge. Three British professors have reported that in terms of economic benefits derived from each thousand cubic meters of water used, these wetlands are at least 32 times more effective than irrigated land.

Governments in most Third World countries remain committed to large-scale projects such as those threatening the Hadejia-Nguru wetlands, but activists hope that their clear-cut economic arguments will help dissuade international aid agencies and Western advisers from promoting them as heavily as they have in the past.

THE NEXT STAGE

It's clear that wetland preservation is a global problem and a controversy that isn't going to go away soon. Much has changed from the days when marshes, swamps, and bogs were denigrated and looked down on as little more than dumping grounds.

Although wetlands have been an issue in the last two presidential campaigns, their fate remains uncertain. Both sides—those who wish to open up privately held wetlands to development and those who want to preserve all possible habitats in their natural state—are supported by strong arguments. Meanwhile, those involved have softened their rhetoric, acknowledging the validity of some of the opposition's views.

One would be hard-pressed to find an advocate of development who wanted to reduce existing parks, refuges, and preserves or cause a bird, fish, or amphibian species to become extinct. Most of them, in fact, acknowledge that wetlands are valuable ecosystems. Instead, they cite society's need for economic growth as a reason to open up some wetlands, especially smaller or marginal ones, to development. They emphasize that the United States and Canada must remain competitive in an increasingly global economy, providing well-paid jobs for their citizens. Continued economic growth is vital if the high standard of living most North Americans enjoy is to be handed down to future generations. Allowing farmers to drain marshes and convert them to fields, or giving builders permits to construct homes, marinas, shops, and offices, is all part of the fuel they say the North American economy requires.

As we have seen, conversion to agricultural use accounts for the majority of wetlands loss. Farmers have become accustomed to dealing with the Soil Conservation Service and other agencies that regulate these habitats. But many small landowners may have bought their property without being aware that it contained designated wetlands; or they may have held the plot for years, since before wetlands were delineated (a process that began only in the 1970s).

These small landowners face a double bind. Regulations prevent them from making the improvements they envisioned, whether it is adding a dock or building on a pristine lot. If they put the property up for sale, restrictions on its future use, called covenants when they are included in the legal papers accompanying the transfer of property, can reduce the price. However, often the landowners are still taxed as if

A Louisiana heron sits on a mangrove tree in the Everglades.

they could reap the maximum economic potential from the land. We may be seeing more property tax rollbacks, such as the Hackensack Meadowlands case in New Jersey described earlier.

Over the last twenty years, wetlands defenders have done a remarkable job of educating the public about the virtues of these once scorned habitats. They have

137

extolled the benefits that swamps, marshes, and bogs provide us—as a home to waterfowl, in flood and pollution control, as cradles of biodiversity, among others. Yet more remains to be done. We have already lost half the wetlands that were on this continent when European colonization began, and, despite this growing public awareness, we still lose hundreds of thousands of more acres each year. In fact, environmentalists regard the fact that the United States continues to lose this much wetland acreage as evidence that regulations are loose and do not need to be relaxed further.

As we all adjust to an increasingly global economy, times can be hard. Events in other parts of the world can result in the closing of a factory down the street. Unemployment is high and many workers need retraining to compete for jobs in growing fields. In the past, environmentalists tended to ignore these so-called bread-and-butter issues, while advocates of unrestricted development used them to garner public support. Now, environmentalists have learned that they must show that creating wildlife refuges and preserving pristine swamps can go hand in hand with ensuring that all citizens have decent jobs and no one goes to bed hungry. By relying on environmental economics, they can point out the measurable benefits our natural heritage provides to society, even when left undisturbed. And, especially in economically depressed areas, wetlands defenders must come up with alternative ways to ensure economic development and job growth.

There is also a need to remain vigilant about the viability of all surviving wetlands, even those preserved by government and private organizations. As we have seen, swamps, marshes, and bogs are fragile ecosystems, whose character can change from one year to another. Environmentalists recognize that education efforts, careful management, and scientific research must all continue—and, in fact, be increased—to maintain biodiversity and preserve the health of wetlands in general.

WHAT YOU CAN DO

If you're interested in helping to save wetlands before more vanish, here are a few things that you can do.

First, find out where there are wetlands in your community. Visit those that are in parks or in preserves and refuges that are open to the public. In order to be an effective advocate for wetlands, it's wise to have learned to appreciate and enjoy them on a first-hand basis. Take along a field guide to aid you in identifying plants and animals. Remember that the pleasures of a wetland often take time to reveal themselves. For instance, you may have to stand in a duck blind next to a marsh for quite some time before a great blue heron comes along. Nevertheless, even when the rewards are subtle, they can be worth waiting for.

Nationwide conservation groups as well as smaller local groups organize hikes and canoe trips to explore wetlands, with an expert guide pointing out interesting features. They also sometimes recruit volunteers to assist in restoring or maintaining these critical habitats.

Work to identify and save wetlands in your own area; a favorite maxim of environmentalists—think globally, act locally—underscores the effectiveness of getting involved in your own backyard. Local chapters of nationwide groups often organize efforts to save wetlands threatened by development, and small ad hoc groups spring up to do so as well. Be on the alert for these activities near you; community bulletin boards, the hometown newspaper, or word of mouth are all good sources of information. Volunteer to help out.

In fact, local zoning boards rule on wetlands development at almost every meeting. The presence of even a few activists to argue against development of a tract of land and stress the advantages of preserving these ecosystems can exert substantial pressure on a local government's decisions. While environmentalists must be vigilant and persistent, they must also learn to work with local officials and landowners in order to save wetlands.

Although a band of organized local residents can act as watchdog over the busy local authorities and agency bureaucrats who are charged with enforcing wetlands policy, it's important to remember that policies themselves are set in state capitals and Washington in the United States, or in provincial capitals and Ottawa in Canada. Join and support nationwide conservation groups; these organizations have lobbied for strong wetlands protections, protested loudly when enforcement was lax, and worked with legislative staffs to draft effective laws. Some groups, such as the Nature Conservancy, also buy tracts of undeveloped land to keep in perpetuity as preserves. The Environmental Defense Fund, the National Audubon Society, Ducks Unlimited, the National Wildlife Federation, and the Sierra Club are just a few of the more prominent groups working to save wetlands. There are many others, but make sure of any group's philosophy and purpose before lending your support: a group whose name implies it works to save wetlands (for instance, the National Wetlands Coalition) may actually be trying to relax wetlands protections.

Finally, the U.S. Fish and Wildlife Service (FWS) sells duck stamps each year. All the proceeds go toward the purchase of new land for wildlife refuges, where waterfowl and other species are ensured unspoiled habitats. Buying duck stamps also enables you to visit national wildlife refuges for free and, if you're interested, to hunt where and when the FWS allows.

Swamps, marshes, and bogs are complicated ecosystems. Their survival involves a series of complex issues, issues that sometimes force society to make difficult decisions about its priorities. In a little over 200 years, more than half the wetlands in the United States have vanished. The specter of development looms over many of those that survive. While perhaps the loss of any one individual wetland may not have enormous side effects, incremental damage occurs whenever a wetland is drained and converted to other uses (for instance, ten such wetlands lost in one country can result in a countywide loss of waterfowl). If we do not work now to preserve wetlands, we may find in the future that it's too late to retrieve the advantages wetlands offer—perhaps waterfowl or fish will have no place to breed, birds no place to rest during migrations, floods will be more severe, water dirtier. Nature is a precious resource that shouldn't be squandered. Without wetlands and other preserves to walk through, ponder, and appreciate, human experience would be deprived of something essential to its well-being.

SOURCE NOTES

Introduction

1. William A. Niering, *Wetlands* (New York: Alfred A. Knopf, 1985): 19.

2. Peter Steinhart, "No Net Loss," *Audubon* 92 (July 1990): 18.

3. T. E. Dahl, *Wetlands Losses in the United States 1780's to 1980's* (Washington, D.C.: U.S. Department of the Interior/Fish and Wildlife Service, 1990): 6.

1. The Types of Wetlands

1. *How Wet Is a Wetland?* (New York and Washington, D.C.: Environmental Defense Fund and World Wildlife Fund, 1992): 9.

2. "Coastal Wetlands," *Sunset* 186 (March 1991): 84.

3. William A. Niering, *Wetlands* (New York: Alfred A. Knopf, 1985): 44–51.

4. *How Wet Is a Wetland?*, 59–60.

5. Niering, *Wetlands*, 89.

6. *How Wet Is a Wetland?*, 81–82.

7. Walter Henricks Hodge, "Where a Heavy Body Is Likely to Sink," *Audubon* 83 (September 1981): 98.

8. Milton Weller, *Freshwater Marshes: Ecology and*

Wildlife Management, 2d ed. (Minneapolis: University of Minnesota Press, 1987): 70.

9. Ibid., 96–100.

2. The Importance of Wetlands

1. Peter Steinhart, "No Net Loss," *Audubon* 92 (July 1990): 18.

2. *How Wet Is a Wetland?* (New York and Washington, D.C.: Environmental Defense Fund and World Wildlife Fund, 1992): 54.

3. Dan Sorenson, "Proponents Say Wildlife Areas Under Siege and Need Protection," *Tucson Citizen,* October 5, 1992, p. 4A.

4. Gregg Easterbrook, "Cleaning Up Our Mess," *Newsweek* 114 (July 24, 1989): 41.

5. *How Wet Is a Wetland?,* xi.

6. J. R. Chambers, "Habitat Degradation and Fishery Declines in the U.S.," Proceedings of the Seventh Symposium on Coastal and Ocean Management, 1991. As cited in *How Wet Is a Wetland?,* 50.

7. *How Wet Is a Wetland?,* 37.

8. John G. Mitchell, "Our Disappearing Wetlands," *National Geographic* 182 (October 1992): 14.

9. Lonnie Williamson, "The Swampbusters," *Outdoor Life* 179 (February 1987): 43.

3. The Flora and Fauna of Wetlands

1. Walter Henricks Hodge, "Where a Heavy Body Is Likely to Sink," *Audubon* 83 (September 1981): 98.

2. William A. Niering, *Wetlands* (New York: Alfred A. Knopf, 1985): 79.

3. William H. Amos and Stephen H. Amos, *Atlantic and Gulf Coasts* (New York: Alfred A. Knopf, 1985): 126–34.

4. Michael Satchell, "Where Have All the Ducks Gone?," *U.S. News and World Report* 105 (October 24, 1988): 72.

5. Janet Lyons and Sandra Jordan, *Walking the Wetlands* (New York: John Wiley, 1989): 175.

6. Ibid., 178.

7. Frank Graham, Jr., "Kite vs. Stork," *Audubon* 92 (May 1990): 108.

8. Niering, *Wetlands,* 78.

9. Lyons and Jordan, *Walking the Wetlands,* 157.

4. The Politics of Preservation

1. Quoted in John Madson, "Green Suits, Gray Suits, and White Hats," *Audubon* 92 (July 1990): 110.

2. *How Wet Is a Wetland?* (New York and Washington, D.C.: Environmental Defense Fund and World Wildlife Fund, 1992): 17.

3. Keith Schneider, "Bush Announces Proposal for Wetlands," *The New York Times,* August 10, 1991, p. 7.

4. Quoted in Charles Campbell, "Bush, Congress Both Roil Waters over Wetlands," *Arizona Daily Star,* September 17, 1991.

5. This study, entitled *How Wet Is a Wetland?*, was published by the Environmental Defense Fund and the World Wildlife Fund. Much of the information in the text that follows is based on chapter 3 of this book.

6. Quoted in Janet Plume, "Rivals Square Off on Battle over Wetlands," *Journal of Commerce and Commercial* 390 (December 16, 1991): 8A.

7. Bill Clinton and Al Gore, *Putting People First: How We Can All Change America* (New York: Times Books, 1992): 96.

8. Keith Schneider, "New Breed of Ecologist to Lead E.P.A.," *The New York Times,* December 17, 1992, p. B20.

9. John G. Mitchell, "The Fable of Pozsgai's Swamp," *Audubon* 92 (July 1990): 113.

5. The Everglades and Other Wetlands

1. Peter Passell, "A Free Enterprise Plan for an

Everglades Cleanup," *The New York Times,* May 1, 1992, p. B18.

2. John Ogden, manager for wildlife research at Everglades National Park, quoted in Frank Graham, Jr., "Kite vs. Stork," *Audubon* 92 (May 1990): 108.

3. Jim Coleman of the National Park Service, quoted in Jon Nordheimer, "The Hurricane's Reshaping of the Landscape Isn't Over," *The New York Times,* September 3, 1992, p. A19.

4. Donald G. Schueler, "Losing Louisiana," *Audubon* 92 (July 1990): 85.

5. Quoted in "Corps of Engineers' Gear-Switching Noted," *Tucson Citizen,* October 7, 1991, p. 4A.

6. Mitigation

1. Interview with Linda van de Vliet (project manager, Storch Engineers, Florham Park, N.J.), June 11, 1992.

2. Quoted in "Coastal Wetlands," *Sunset* 186 (March 1991): 90.

3. Quoted in John G. Mitchell, "Our Disappearing Wetlands," *National Geographic* 182 (October 1992): 45.

7. The Future of Wetlands

1. Marlise Simons, "The Wetlands Home of Many Species Threatened by Spain's Great Thirst," *The New York Times,* May 27, 1992, p. A3.

2. Fred Pearce, "Death of an Oasis," *Audubon* 94 (May 1992): 70.

GLOSSARY

Aquifer: A level of water lying below the surface of the soil. This is the source for much drinking water in North America. The *water table* is the top of the aquifer.

Biodiversity: A concept stressing that any ecosystem or habitat contains a multitude of plant and animal species, each of which is a part contributing to the good of the whole.

Bog: A type of wetland featuring a mat of Sphagnum moss and other vegetation that slowly accumulates on top of a basin of mineral-poor, oxygen-deprived, acidic water. Generally, a bog has no stream running into it, nor is there any outflow of water.

Bottomlands: Low-lying areas that are likely to be classified as wetlands.

Bromeliad: A family of plants that, lacking roots, take in moisture and nutrients from rain and the air. Found only in warm regions, bromeliads live on tree trunks and on the uppermost leaves of trees.

Coniferous: Used to describe a tree that bears cones. Most coniferous trees are evergreens and do not shed their leaves all at once in the fall.

146

Corm: The bulblike section of the roots of some plants, found immediately below the stem.

Covenant: A legally binding restriction of the future use of a piece of land.

Cypress swamp: A type of swamp dominated by the bald cypress or pond cypress tree. Cypress swamps are found in the southeastern United States, concentrated along the Atlantic coast, in Florida, along the Gulf of Mexico, and along the Mississippi River as far north as Kentucky.

Dabblers: Ducks that usually search for food by standing in shallow water and sticking their beaks in to fish out plants or small animals. Among the dabblers are the gadwall, mallard, and northern shoveler. By contrast, diving ducks swim underwater to find food.

Deciduous: Used to describe a tree that sheds its leaves in the fall.

Delineation: The process of mapping out the boundaries of a recognized wetland, using criteria based on government guidelines.

Delta: The area at the mouth of a river that has been built up over the years by deposits of sediment that the river has carried with it from upstream.

Detritus: Dead plant matter that has begun to decompose.

Draining: The act of removing water from a wetland, usually as part of conversion to farmland or other uses. Often followed by *filling in,* which is adding soil to the drained area. Filling in of wetlands requires a permit from the Army Corps of Engineers.

Dredging: The act of removing soil from a wetland in order to create deeper water. Usually done to create larger areas of open water, including irrigation canals, navigable channels, or marinas.

Eat-out: The consumption of virtually all plants in a marsh by an exploding population of muskrats, resulting in new, large patches of open water.

147

Ecosystem: A natural environment considered as a complex whole that functions as a unit.

Effluent: Treated wastewater that is then discharged into a natural body of water. The word can also refer to any pollutant discharged into the environment.

Emergents: Plants that grow partly in water and partly out of water, such as sedges.

Enhancement: The process of improving a wetland's quality by adding soils or vegetation specially adapted to thrive in such a habitat.

Epiphyte: A plant that usually grows on another plant and takes in moisture and nutrients from the air or from rain, and not through a root system.

Estivation: A period when an animal is inactive because of drought and/or extreme heat.

Estuary: An area where salt and fresh water mix, typically at the mouth of a river.

Eutrophication: The process by which a body of water, such as a lake, becomes overloaded with dissolved nutrients (such as phosphate) and deprived of oxygen.

Exotic: A plant or animal species that has been introduced into an ecosystem that is not its native habitat. Examples of exotics include the melaleuca tree in south Florida and the nutria in Louisiana. Because exotics lack natural predators in their new habitats, their population grows rapidly.

Facultative species: One of four classifications of plants that analyze the species' favored habitat as it relates to wetland status. Classifying vegetation in this manner is a method used in determining whether a particular area is a wetland. The four classifications are *obligate species,* which is short for obligatory wetlands species (these plants are virtually always found in wetlands, never in uplands); *facultative-wetland species* (plants that appear primarily in wetlands); *facultative species* (plants that grow equally well in wetlands and uplands); and *facultative-upland species* (plants that are typically found in uplands and appear less than one-third of the time in wetlands).

Facultative-upland species: *See* Facultative species.

Facultative-wetland species: *See* Facultative species.

Fen: A type of bog that has some water inflow, from a brook or small river.

Filling in: *See* Draining.

Floating aquatics: Plants whose leaves float on the surface of the water. Usually found in deeper marshes, they may float freely on the surface, without any root at all, or they may have a long leaf stalk, or petiole, stretching down to the base of the marsh.

Flood peak: The highest point water reaches during a flood.

Floodplain: The area alongside a river or other body of water that is subject to flooding.

Food chain: The group of living things in a habitat classified by what eats what and likened to links in a chain. A organism will feed on the link below it, and be eaten in turn by the link above it.

Hammock: An area in the Everglades where the ground level is raised above the level of the "river of grass"; usually home to a grove of tropical trees.

Head: A small raised area in the Everglades, typically home to a couple of willow or bay trees. Hammocks are larger than heads.

Herbivore: An animal that eats only vegetation.

Hydric soil: Soil that is saturated or flooded for long parts of the growing season.

Hydrology: The science dealing with water and its properties on the surface of the land, underground, and in the air. With soil and vegetation, hydrology considerations are one of the three ways in which wetland status is determined.

Hydrophyte: A plant that can grow in soil that is too

149

waterlogged and/or oxygen deficient for most other plants to survive.

Insectivorous: Used to describe an animal that eats primarily insects.

Intertidal flats: Flat areas that are covered by high tide and exposed at low tide. Also called mud flats, they are sometimes classified as nonvegetated wetlands.

Levee: A man-made embankment on a riverbank to prevent flooding.

Mangrove swamp: A type of coastal wetland found in subtropical and tropical regions, such as Florida. Dominated by mangrove trees, mangrove swamps replace the coastal saltwater marshes found in more temperate parts of North America.

Marsh: A type of wetland dominated by soft-stemmed vegetation such as cattails, reeds, and sedges.

Mitigation: The process of compensating for man-made damage to a wetland by enhancing, restoring, or creating another similar habitat nearby.

Mitigation banking: A system whereby parties who successfully enhance, restore, or create wetlands earn credits. The credits are then made available for sale to developers who wish to build on wetlands but cannot find a mitigation project of their own.

Monoculture: The system of growing only one crop in a given area.

Mycorrhizae: Acid-loving soil fungi that live in the roots of some orchids and enable them to survive in bogs.

Obligate species: *See* Facultative species.

Omnivore: An animal that eats both plants and other animals.

Peat: The compacted layers of Sphagnum moss and other dead vegetative matter often found underneath the mat of a bog. Peat can be harvested, dried, and then burned as fuel; it is also used commercially to pack garden plants during transport.

Petiole: The part of the leaf that resembles a stalk and leads from the stem.

Pneumatophores: The aerial roots of the black mangrove tree.

Pocosin: A type of shrub swamp found in Virginia and the Carolinas, usually on slightly elevated land.

Prairie pothole: A type of marsh found on the prairies of the upper Midwest and the Canadian plains. Found in basins formed at the end of the last Ice Age, prairie potholes can be temporary, seasonal, semipermanent, or permanent. Prairie potholes are home to the majority of North American ducks during the nesting and breeding seasons.

Property rights movement: A coalition of property owners who believe that wetlands laws and other restrictions on development are too restrictive in telling them what they can do with their land. Also called the *wise use movement.*

Riparian wetland: Any wetland that lies alongside a river.

Shrub swamp: A swamp dominated by shrubs such as alder and pussy willows. Most common in the upper Midwest and the Southeast, shrub swamps are often transitional as a habitat evolves from being more marshlike to more swamplike.

Slough: A small, sluggish creek in a marsh or tidal flat, often the only place with standing water during dryer periods.

Sphagnum moss: The type of moss characteristically found in bogs.

Submergents: Wetlands plants that live entirely in the water, with their roots in the marsh or pond bottom and their leaves beneath the surface of the water.

Swamp: A type of wetland dominated by trees or shrubs.

Taking: The acquisition of private property by the government without just compensation; banned in the United States by the Fifth Amendment.

Upland: Land that is not wetland.

Water table: *See* Aquifer.

Waterfowl: Birds that spend a significant portion of their lives in wetlands or in or at the edge of lakes, rivers, or streams.

Wet meadow: A type of freshwater marsh that looks much like a grassy meadow. Although it lacks the areas of open water typical of most marshes, it does have saturated soil.

Wetlands: Natural habitats such as swamps, marshes, or bogs where the presence of water at or just beneath the surface results in the dominance of particular kinds of characteristic vegetation.

Wise use movement: *See* Property rights movement.

FOR FURTHER READING

Books

Amos, William H., and Stephen H. Amos. *Atlantic and Gulf Coasts.* New York: Alfred A. Knopf, 1985.

Borgioli, Alessandro, and Giuliano Cappelli. *The Living Swamp.* London: Orbis Publishing, 1979.

Douglas, Marjory Stoneman. *The Everglades: River of Grass.* Sarasota, Fla.: Pineapple Press, 1988. (A reprint of the 1947 edition.)

Feierabend, J. Scott, and John M. Zelazny. *Status Report on Our Nation's Wetlands.* Washington, D.C.: National Wildlife Federation, 1987.

Goldman-Carter, Jan. *A Citizen's Guide to Protecting Wetlands.* Washington, D.C.: National Wildlife Federation, 1989.

How Wet Is a Wetland?: The Impact of the Proposed Revisions to the Federal Wetlands Delineation Manual. New York and Washington, D.C.: Environmental Defense Fund and World Wildlife Fund, 1992.

Lyons, Janet, and Sandra Jordan. *Walking the Wetlands.* New York: John Wiley, 1989.

Niering, William A. *Wetlands.* New York: Alfred A. Knopf, 1985.

Teal, John, and Mildred Teal. *Life and Death of the Salt Marsh.* New York: Ballantine, 1983.

Periodicals

"Coastal Wetlands." *Sunset* 186 (March 1991): 82–90.

Dupleix, Nicole. "South Florida Water: Paying the Price." *National Geographic* 178 (July 1990): 89–112.

Easterbrook, Gregg. "Cleaning Up Our Mess." *Newsweek* 114 (July 24, 1989): 26–42.

Graham, Frank, Jr. "Kite vs. Stork." *Audubon* 92 (May 1990): 104–10.

Hodge, Walter Henricks. "Where a Heavy Body Is Likely to Sink." *Audubon* 83 (September 1981): 98–110.

Holloway, Marguerite. "High and Dry." *Scientific American* 265 (December 1991): 16–20.

Laycock, George. "How to Save a Wetland." *Audubon* 92 (July 1990): 97–101. (Wetlands were the theme of this issue, which contains six other articles on various facets of the topic.)

Mitchell, John G. "Our Disappearing Wetlands," *National Geographic* 182 (October 1992): 3–45.

Passell, Peter. "A Free Enterprise Plan for an Everglades Cleanup," *The New York Times,* May 1, 1992.

Pearce, Fred. "Death of an Oasis." *Audubon* 94 (May 1992): 66–74.

Price, J. William. "The Marsh That Arcata Built." *Sierra* 72 (May–June 1987): 51–53.

Raver, Anne. "Let Us Now Praise Famous Swamps." *The New York Times Magazine,* August 18, 1991, 21 ff.

Robbins, William. "For Farmers, Wetlands Mean a Legal Quagmire." *The New York Times,* April 24, 1990.

Schueler, Donald. "That Sinking Feeling." *Sierra* 75 (January–February 1990): 42–50.

Sorenson, Dan. "Riparian Zones: Lifeblood of the Desert." *Tucson Citizen,* October 5, 6, and 7, 1992.

Stevens, William K. "Economists Strive to Find Environment's Bottom Line." *The New York Times,* September 8, 1992.

————. "Restoring Lost Wetland: It's Possible but Not Easy." *The New York Times,* October 29, 1991.

Stewart, Doug. "Nothing Goes to Waste in Arcata's Teeming Marshes." *Smithsonian* 21 (April 1990): 174–79.

Yates, Steve. "Marjory Stoneman Douglas and the Glades Crusades." *Audubon* 85 (March 1983): 113–27.

INDEX

opposition to, 89, 91, 97–98, 99–102, 110
permits, 90, 121–22
state laws, 85
students' role, 139–40
See also Mitigation projects
Property-rights movement, 100–102

Quayle, Dan, 91

Rabbits, 79–80
Raccoons, 77, *78*, 79
Rails, 68, 70
Recreation, 41, *42*
Red maple trees, 22, 54
Reilly, William, 97
Reptiles, 80–83
Riparian wetlands, 19, *124*
Riverlands project, 119–20

Salamanders, 80
Shrubs, 23–24, 27
Small landowners, 99–102, 136–37
Snail kites, 70–71, 111
Snakes, 80
Soil conservation, 43
Soil Conservation Service, 86–87, *88*
Soldado estuary, 133–34
Spanish moss, 47, *49*
Sphagnum mosses, *25*, 26, 27, 54, 56

Spruce trees, 29
Submergents, 18
Sugar industry, 107, 110
Sundews, 56
Swampbuster law, 87
Swamps, 13, 22
northern, 22, 72–73
shrub, 23–24
southern, 23
western, 24

Taxes, 100–101, 136–37
Touch-me-not, 56
Transitional environments, 10
Trees. *See specific names.*
Turtles, *36*, 80

Venus's-flytrap, 56–57

Washington, George, 11
Water lilies, 57, *58*
Wetlands
change in, 30–32
classifying, 13–14, 30
features of, 10, 13
loss of, 11–12, 19–20, 39, 85, 86–87, 141
productivity of, 32–33
valuation of, 43–45
Wet meadows, 18
White cedar trees, 57
Whooping cranes, 71
Wood storks, 70–71, 111

Zedler, Joy, 127

ABOUT THE AUTHOR

Trent Duffy is a writer and editor who has had extensive experience in publishing. He lives and works in New York City.

574.5
DUF

Duffy, Trent.

The vanishing
wetlands.

$13.79

DATE DUE	BORROWER'S NAME	ROOM NO

574.5
DUF

Duffy, Trent.

The vanishing
wetlands.

HIGHLAND HIGH SCHOOL LIBRARY
MONTEREY, VA